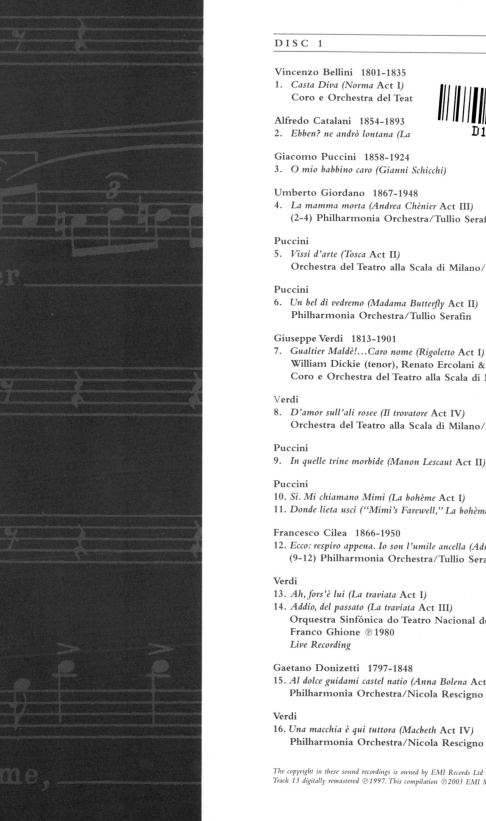

Maria Callas

Maria Callas

A MUSICAL
BIOGRAPHY

ROBERT LEVINE

BLACK DOG
& LEVENTHAL
PUBLISHERS
NEW YORK

The enclosed compact disc compilation ℗ 2003
EMI Music Special Markets Manufactured by EMI Music Special Markets,
1750 North Vine Street, Hollywood, California 90028.
72438-26772-2-2

Libretti reproduced by courtesy of Angel/EMI Classics.

ISBN 1-57912-283-3

Library of Congress Cataloging-in-Publication Data
on file at Black Dog & Leventhal Publishers, Inc.

Cover and interior design: Liz Driesbach, edstudio

Book manufactured in the U.S.A.

Published by
Black Dog & Leventhal Publishers, Inc.
151 West 19th Street
New York, New York 10011

Distributed by
Workman Publishing Company
708 Broadway
New York, New York 10003

g f e d c b a

PHOTO CREDITS

Archivio Editoriale Gli Olmi: 13, 15, 16, 20, 23, 24, 28t, 28b, 29, 30, 34, 37, 38, 40, 43,
45, 46, 50, 51, 54, 59, 60, 64, 71, 77, 79, 92, 93, 94, 95, 98, 106, 128, 145, 158, 184, 187

Bettmann/Corbis: frontis, 156

Courtesy of EMI Classics: 76, 88, 108

EMI Classics/Claude Poirier: 86, 161

EMI Classics/Maurice Harrington: 70

EMI Classics/Publifoto: 10, 108

Lebrecht: 114

Lyric Opera of Chicago: 66, 68, 75, 90, 124, 148,

Mondadori Press: 122

Courtesy of Palacio de Bellas Artes, Mexico: 48, 150-151, 127

Photofest: 21l, 221r, 57, 63, 89, 96, 97, 100, 105, 111, 113, 114, 115, 116, 117, 119, 130, 137, 140, 192

Publifoto, 174, 178

Courtesy of Teatro Colon, Buenos Aires: 47

Teatro alla Scala: 44, 58, 60, 61, 62, 65, 73, 81, 82, 83, 85, 120, 121, 132,
141, 153 164, 166, 167, 171, 179, 194, 196, 198, 200l, 200r.

V & A Picture Library: 99, 101

TRANSLATION CREDITS

Disc 1
Track 3 Translation © G. Ricordi & Co., Milan
Track 11 Translation William Weaver © Capitol Records Inc. 1952
Track 12 Translation © Angel Records USA 1968
Track 15 Translation © Willliam Ashbrook

Disc 2
Track 4 Translation © Capitol Records 1961
Track 5 © Gwyn Morris 1976

Acknowledgments

The author would like to thank Paul Harrington for his patience, superb researching, and gleaning; Laura Ross for-and-despite her red pen, Constance Sayre for knowing everything and being willing to share it and help, Nell Mulderry at EMI for locating, putting together, and figuring out, the BD&L crew - Iris Bass, Liz Driesbach, Dara Lazar, and True Sims - who made the book clean and good looking, and, as usual, J.P. Leventhal, who, in an arid time, remains a geyser of great ideas.

—ROBERT LEVINE

The publisher would like to thank the following people for their help in obtaining the photographs: Roberto Allegri at Editoriale Gli Olmi, Deborah Milardi at Mondadori Press, Malcolm Gordon at Photofest, Jemal Creary at Corbis Images, Rosa DiSalvo at Getty Images, Elena Fumagalli at Teatro la Scala, Roger Pines at the Lyric Opera of Chicago, and Matthew Pritchard for translation and correspondence.

Contents

DISC 2

Maria Callas

CHAPTER 1

An Extraordinary Life

Most years have their highlights and 1923 seems to have been awash with them. To name a few: the "Beer Hall Putsch" in Munich, which led to Adolf Hitler's imprisonment, the publication of his autobiography and manifesto, Mein Kampf; President Warren G. Harding's death in San Francisco after a sudden illness; the ascension of Rin Tin Tin as the world's first canine film star; and *Time* magazine's debut.

But everyone has his or her focus, and if you are, or ever have been, interested in opera, followed Jet-Set gossip in the '50s and '60s or paid attention to international culture, one event stands out—the birth, in New York City, of Maria Anna Sophia Cecilia Kalogeropolous, who would grow up to be known to the world as Maria Callas, "La Divina." This might seem like hyperbole, but there have been few artists in the past one hundred years who have had such a profound influence not only in their chosen medium, but far beyond. Indeed, the stresses and strains of her glamorous life are now as legendary as the epic performances that propelled her to fame.

Operatically dramatic statements aside, the facts begin here: On December 2nd (or 4th),

1923, Maria Anna Sophie Cecilia was born to George and Evangelia Kalogeropoulos. The couple had only been in the United States since August, after emigrating from their native Greece. George was a pharmacist who had built a very successful business in his native land. The handsome, debonair young man had established himself quickly, and seemingly sought greater challenges. This was all a great surprise to Evangelia for several reasons. To begin with she was a woman of great ambition, and despite his good looks and success, Evangelia had become disenchanted with her husband soon after their marriage. It may have been his womanizing, it may have been that he did not have the same desire for luxury that she did, but whatever it was, she did as was expected of a Greek woman of the time and assumed the role of the good wife. Their first child, a daughter they called Jackie, was born in 1917, and in 1920 a son, Vasily, was born. Vasily seemed to bring the couple together as nothing since their earliest days together had. Even given the significance first sons typically have in Greek families, the intensity of their love for him and the manner in which it rekindled their relationship suggests that they were seeking some fix for their marriage. Unfortunately, the baby was one of the first victims of a typhoid fever outbreak in their hometown, Meligala, in early 1923. Just as the little boy's birth had brought George and Evangelia together, his death created an emotional void between them. It is understandable, then, how much they hoped the child to be born in December of the same year would be a boy.

Of course, this was not to be the case. She was so distraught by having borne a girl, Evangelia refused to see Maria for the first four days of her life. She and George had been so certain that the child would be a boy that all of the baby clothes she had knitted were blue, and they had never even considered what name they might give to a girl. When the nurse asked them what to put on the hospital bracelet, Evangelia blurted out "Sophia" and George countered with "Cecilia," but they eventually agreed on Maria. At her christening at the Greek Orthodox cathedral on East Seventy-fourth Street, all of these names and another were given to her: Maria Anna Sophia Cecilia. It was not long afterwards that George officially changed the family name to Callas, in an effort to fit in better in America.

In 1929, with help from Leonidas Lantzounis, a longtime family friend, George was able to set up his own pharmacy in Manhattan's Washington Heights. Dr. Lantzounis had left Meligala a year before the Kalogeropolous family. It was he who had been at the docks to welcome them when they stepped off the steamship, and it was he who brought Maria to Evangelia when she was born, and who would became her godfather. Not only was he an active supporter of the family in these early days, he went on to play a vital role for Maria throughout her life. By this time the Callas family had moved from a cramped apartment in Astoria, Queens, to 192nd Street in Manhattan. George's

Maria with her mother Evangelia and sister Jackie at home in Athens, 1937. The attention lavished upon her elegant older sister cemented Maria's determination to achieve greatness.

growing success had enabled Evangelia to create a much more comfortable home in the larger house, and as a symbol of their financial well-being they acquired a Pianola. This instrument had extra significance for Evangelia, as it reminded her of her grandfather, a hero of the Greek Army known as the "Singing Commander" during the Balkan War. Crowds of people would gather around his porch and beg him to sing arias like "*Questa o quella*" from *Rigoletto*. Although she did not have the musical talent of her grandfather, Evangelia had always wanted to be an actress, but given her provincial upbringing, she never had the opportunity. She would not allow her daughters to miss such opportunities and would be sure that the girls were well prepared to take advantage of them.

Accordingly, not long after the Pianola was acquired, a Gramophone appeared. This would cause problems of its own, however, as the first records Evangelia purchased were Tosca's *"Vissi d'arte,"* and arias from *Martha* and *Aida*. George, not sharing his wife's cultural interests, bought recordings of Greek pop songs. Soon, there were regular clashes over what they would listen to. These rows characterized the long-standing problems in their marriage: They were at best lower middle class, and Evangelia's ambitious nature would never allow her to forget the higher social position of her family in Greece, while George seemed satisfied with the relative success he had built in America. To his mind it was enough to have a little business and a minor position in the Greek immigrant community, and plenty of ladies to romance on the side. While they could certainly have lived a comfortable enough life, it was not enough for Evangelia, and she focused on ensuring that her daughters' tastes would not be corrupted by George's.

Meanwhile, Jackie and Maria weathered their stormy home life and managed as best they could. There were five and a half years between them, but that was not the only gulf. Besides being the older, Jackie was a beautiful little girl. Maria, who had been twelve and a half pounds when born, remained heavy set, a problem that plagued her into adulthood and had a profound effect

on her career. As a child, she was simply fat and plain. Evangelia doted on Jackie, and given the push and pull within the family, it seems clear that this was one of the things that drove Maria toward such artistic heights later in life.

Musicality Emerges

It was crucial to Evangelia that her daughters get involved in the arts. While Jackie was physically blessed and, in her mother's eyes, could do little wrong, Maria must have felt that beyond taking joy in her mother's cooking, she had to do something to merit her affection. There are many family stories of Maria's musicality from these very earliest years, tales of her babyish yet seemingly musical warblings from the crib, and of the slightly older Maria crouching under the Pianola ecstatically listening to the "music" she made as she played with the instrument's pedals. Clearly their rivalry was behind the frequent fights between the two children, but Maria idolized her sister, and this led to an incident in 1929 that nearly cost her her life.

That July, Maria was waiting with her parents to cross the street to their house when she saw Jackie standing on the other side. Maria broke away from Evangelia and ran into the traffic. She was hit by a car and dragged twenty-five feet. At St. Elizabeth's Hospital, George and Evangelia were first told that her chances of survival were not good, but they were soon assured that Maria would recover and, after twenty-two days in the hospital, she was released. Afterwards she was prone to accidents, more irritable, and tended to get into various misadventures, but there did not appear to be any lasting effects from that dramatic accident. And as bad as that crash was, the Great Stock Market Crash a few months later would, as it did to so many, cause even greater hardship and change in the family.

George was forced to sell his pharmacy and, between October of 1929 and 1933, the family had to move several times. Even as their apartments shrank, however, Evangelia's commitment to her daughters' musical education remained strong. George became a traveling salesman for a pharmaceutical company in order to make ends meet, and his wife's constant reminders of the prestigious family life she had left behind in Greece rang in his ears. George, never having had much of an appreciation for high culture, thought it a dangerous luxury to spend so much of his hard-earned income on piano lessons three times a week for each daughter. It was in this environment that Maria began her musical education in 1930.

To say that Evangelia was the traditional show-biz mom is a bit of an understatement. One of her fondest memories was of Maria when she was ten. On a warm May evening, Maria was at the piano playing and singing *"La Paloma,"* when Evangelia looked out the window and noticed that there was a crowd of people listening from the street outside the apartment. Maria's performance was greeted with raucous applause and when the crowd finally

The Kalogeropoulos family in 1937. From left to right: Sister Jackie, mother Evangelia Dimitriadis, father George, and Maria.

dispersed, doubtless Evangelia could not help but think of her own childhood evenings on her grandfather's porch. It cemented her resolve that Maria would fulfill the destiny that she herself was denied.

Not long after she began her lessons, Maria was entered in contests and talent shows of all sorts, as well as taking the lead in school plays and solo roles in concerts. Despite all of this, Maria talked about becoming a dentist. To observe the Callas girls during this period it would have been impossible to believe that a public, glamorous life was in Maria's future. The Maria destined to become "La Divina" was overweight, pimply and wore thick spectacles, while Jackie was slim and attractive with deep brown eyes and chestnut hair. In spite of the evidence of Maria's budding talent, it seemed a surer bet that charming Jackie would marry well and be taken care of, while her younger sister would be a maiden aunt at best, and need that unglamorous career in dentistry. (In those days, it was generally assumed that a girl pursued a career only because she could not marry successfully.) Maria would later say that she had been "an ugly duckling, fat, clumsy and unpopular." With her father, who even at his best could be oddly disinterested, focusing on making ends meet in these very hard times, and in the shadow of her sister, she turned to the pursuit of her mother's dreams as a means of getting the attention and approval she needed.

The beginning of the realization of her mother's drive for fame—and her own drive for her mother's affection—came when Maria was eleven. Singing *"La Paloma"* once again, she won first place in a national amateur talent contest on the Mutual Radio Network. The first prize was a Bulova watch. Her second public appearance was in another talent show broadcast from Chicago. Although she came in second this time, the fact that it was the very popular Jack Benny who emceed the event was more than compensation. Thus began a period of her life that presaged Maria's life to come, in which she was involved in a seemingly ceaseless cycle of talent contests, children's programs and radio shows. Through her participation in these, as exhausting as they were, Maria developed a sense of destiny around her singing. One Saturday after

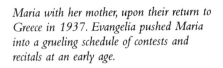

Maria with her mother, upon their return to Greece in 1937. Evangelia pushed Maria into a grueling schedule of contests and recitals at an early age.

noon she was listening to a radio broadcast of the Metropolitan Opera's performance of *Lucia di Lammermoor*, with Lily Pons singing Lucia. Halfway through the Mad Scene, Maria began angrily motioning towards the radio and shouting that Pons had strayed off-pitch. When a visiting friend who witnessed this chastised her for criticizing a star of the Met, Maria quickly retorted, "I don't care if she is a star. She sings off-key. Just wait and see, one day I'm going to be a star myself, a bigger star than her."

"Totally Greek"

By 1936 Evangelia decided that if her children were going to attain the lofty ambitions she had for them, they must return to Greece. It is interesting to note that even then, despite Jackie's more obvious charms and advantages, Maria's budding successes on the stage seemed to confirm for her mother that it was Maria who had the best chance to achieve greatness. George barely fought his wife's plan to take his daughters away from him. The two clearly recognized that this separation would not only be better for their children, but for them as well. Evangelia's family and their connections in Greece would be of great help, and it would be much cheaper for them to live. In fact George probably viewed this separation as something of a release. Maria graduated from eighth grade in January of 1936, after a well-received performance in the ceremonial production of Gilbert

and Sullivan's *HMS Pinafore*. It not only marked the first of many staged musical performances, it was the end of her formal education.

Jackie had left for Greece several weeks earlier, so Maria was alone with her mother and their three canaries when they boarded the Italian ocean liner, *Saturnia*, only a short time after her graduation ceremony. Maria spent the first few days of the journey seasick, but she gradually recovered and, to pass the time, she sang. After warming up in the cabin with the canaries, she would go into the tourist lounge and sing there. One evening after hearing her perform, the captain asked Maria to sing at the Sunday church service. So taken was he with her that he followed that invitation with another to sing at a party he was giving for two Italian contessas and his officers. Singing in the chapel had been an honor; the opportunity to sing before the handsome officers and aristocrats from First Class was something else.

Understandably, Maria was nervous the day of the party. When the time came, the plump little girl in a simple white-collared blue dress sat down at the piano to accompany herself and took off her glasses. She sang her two favorites, "*La Paloma*" and "Ave Maria," and finished off with the Habanera from *Carmen*. As she sang Carmen's final lines, "*Et si je t'aime, prends garde à toi,*" she grabbed a carnation from a vase near the piano and threw it to the captain, just as the character Carmen would do in a staged performance. This final flourish charmed her audience, particularly the captain, who kissed the flower, and when he thanked her afterwards, returned the favor by giving her a bouquet and a doll. He was clearly taken by this child with the extraordinarily developed sense of drama to go along with her remarkable voice. When the *Saturnia* finally arrived in Patras, the Captain and his officers met Maria and Evangelia at the quay to wish their charming little diva-to-be luck. The doll that the captain gave her was the first doll she had ever had. Evangelia did not approve of such frivolous things. Maria held on to this keepsake throughout her stay in Athens.

Greece was everything that Maria could have hoped for. She loved the beautiful weather in her parents' native land and her first days there were magically free of the regimentation and discipline that would come to define her life in the coming years. She later said that the glory of the blue Aegean, the white clouds against the blue Spring sky and the silver-gray olive trees were such a contrast to the cement and brick that she had grown up surrounded by in New York that it confirmed her sense that, "My blood is pure Greek...I feel totally Greek."

Evangelia, meanwhile, was also pleased to be back in her element. Dressed in the height of New York fashion, she cut an impressive figure before her family and old friends. They were impressed with the stories of Maria's prizes and successes. It was Evangelia's intention to use her family's social position to aid Maria. Soon Maria was taking part in a seemingly endless series of auditions, which meant that she would sing for anyone her mother convinced to stay still for a

few moments. Despite all of this, the support Evangelia had hoped for was not forthcoming. The family was pleased to have them back from America, but being a singer was not quite the social pinnacle to them that it was to Evangelia. Furthermore, musical talent was not such a rarity in this family. Sure, Grandfather Petros was known as the "Singing Colonel," but the most significant thing here was that he was a colonel, not a singer. Maria's Uncle Efthimios's singing voice was quite renowned as well, yet even his support was tempered as he told Evangelia, "Don't push her too fast. She's only a little girl. She's in a new country with a new family. Let her get used to us. Then I'll arrange an audition for her."

In the six months or so before Efthimios got Maria her audition, Evangelia and the girls moved out of her mother's into a nearby, furnished house and they began to settle in. By the time September came and her uncle used his contacts at the Royal Theater to arrange an audition, Maria had begun to adjust. The audition was with Maria Trivella, a teacher from the National Conservatory, and on that day Maria experienced the same feeling she would have before every performance of her life: panic. Evangelia's own fears could only have heightened her daughter's, as she nervously helped Maria into her white organdy dress. With the arrival of Maria's grandmother, two aunts and Uncle Efthimios, who would attend the audition along with Jackie and her mother, the panic deepened. Maria later described this state, "Before

I sing I know nothing, don't remember the part, don't know where I start. It is panic not knowing one thing before you go onstage."

Despite her state of mind, Maria gave a spectacular performance. "This is talent!" exclaimed Maria Trivella, who immediately agreed to take Maria as a student of both singing and French. She then helped Maria get a scholarship from the conservatory, for which she conspired with Evangelia to falsify Maria's age. Luckily for Maria the authorities were more than willing to believe that she was sixteen rather than thirteen, and they agreed to subsidize her entire musical education.

Mentors and Magic

This was the beginning of the first of several periods in Maria's life dominated by one influential person. Maria Trivella became much more to the thirteen-year-old than just a mentor. Indeed, she took the place of Evangelia and instilled far greater confidence in Maria than the girl could ever have gotten from her mother. Her entire focus became music. There were days when Maria had lunch in Trivella's studio, and often Evangelia would serve her dinner in her bedroom, so that she could continue working with the plate on her lap. The focus on her career in this early period came back to haunt her later in life when she realized how much she had given over to music, but at the time, music made her feel that she was more than an

overweight, pimply, myopic girl with a domineering mother.

Maria's impressive willpower and focus enabled her to develop into the artist we think of when we think of Callas, but at the time her fellow students were hardly charmed by her chilly single-mindedness. One of them later said that "her earnestness was oppressive." Maria knew, however, that it was necessary to focus her talent into a light that would outshine everyone else. It was Maria against the world, and she would not share the spotlight. Of course, the anger and alienation that she had long felt were elements of this drive, but as time went on she achieved the calm, regal demeanor for which she would become known. A close friend later revealed, "When I was near Maria, her appearance may have been of calm and silence, but if I sat near her quietly, without talking, I never felt calm or silence coming from her. Deep down the turmoil was hidden. On the surface everything was quiet; underneath I felt the volcano getting ready to explode at any minute."

During this early phase of her life, Maria was crafting that convincing facade. "I work: therefore I am," she told Kenneth Harris in an interview for *The Observer* many years later. Several days before her fifteenth birthday, she made her debut singing Santuzza in a student production of Mascagni's *Cavalleria rusticana*. Her focus was on winning first prize in opera at the conservatory, and she knew that it depended upon her performance in this show. With the force of her youth and her flair for the dramatic, she announced

Maria (kneeling in front of her mother) with some acquaintances on a trip to Saloniko, Greece, in 1943. Though a respected student at the National Conservatory, Maria rarely associated with her fellow students.

to her mother that if she did not take the prize she would quit the stage. Maria did win, and the audience's ringing applause confirmed what she already knew: opera was her destiny.

While her work kept her happy through the years in Athens before the start of World War II, her beautiful older sister was an ever-present reminder of everything that Maria was not. At twenty-two, Jackie, slender, tall, beautiful and personable, had acquired a boyfriend, Milton Embiricos. Milton was the son of well-to-do shipping family, and the two were engaged in the summer of 1939. It was just a few short months after Mussolini had marched into Albania and established a fascist government bordering Greece, but there was little thought of war as the family celebrated the engagement with a trip to the island of Corfu on Milton's yacht. As they enjoyed the Grand Hotel and the costly gifts that Milton showered upon them, Evangelia and the rest of the family virtually ignored Maria. Still fat and awkward, Maria could not help but feel out of place, and she yearned for their "special" holiday to come to an end. Once again she had only to see her sister's successes to be reminded of the struggles before her. The timing was just right, therefore, for Maria to meet the woman who would take Maria Trivella's place as a guide in her life, Elvira de Hidalgo.

The de Hidalgo period would probably not have come if not for the war. A Spaniard, Elvira de Hidalgo was an established soprano who

was known not only in Athens but at the Met, La Scala and Covent Garden. De Hidalgo had fallen in love with Greece in earlier visits and had taken a teaching position at the Odeon Athenon, Athens' leading conservatory. Evangelia had heard that de Hidalgo was at the Odeon and was able to arrange an audition with her for Maria. She did not make much of an impression upon de Hidalgo. The sight of what appeared to be an average, awkward, overweight teenager did not inspire the teacher's interest, and as she said, "The idea of that girl wanting to become a singer was laughable." But Maria's voice and

Elvira de Hidalgo at home, 1960s.

Callas's teacher, Elvira de Hidalgo, circa 1914. "Maria abused her God-given gifts," Hidalgo once remarked.

performance were remarkable. De Hidalgo closed her eyes and reveled in the "violent cascades of sound, full of drama and emotion." The teacher could hear in the young girl's performance what her voice could one day be, and, indeed, what sort of star she might become with proper training. Maria was immediately admitted to the conservatory tuition-free, as de Hidalgo's personal student.

From that point on, Maria was at de Hidalgo's studio every morning at 10:00 A.M. and would stay through the day, sitting in on other students' classes when her own were complete. She had begun the long and at times painful process of learning bel canto. When she started, her range was so narrow that many teachers at the conservatory considered her a mezzo, rather than a soprano. Under de Hidalgo she began developing high notes and low chest notes that she had never used before. Maria would describe this in later years as a physical process. "I was like an athlete, who enjoys using and developing his muscles, like the youth who runs and jumps, enjoying and growing at the same time, like the girl who dances, enjoying the dance for its own sake and learning to dance at the same time." Bel canto was not simply "beautiful singing" to de Hidalgo, and Maria would later echo her teacher when she defined it as "a specific training of the voice, the development of a technique for making full use of it as a player of the violin or the flute is trained to make full use of his instrument." As she expanded her voice she learned a deep, broad range of roles that in time would be defined as hers; in fact, she learned them even before her voice was developed enough to sing them. De Hidalgo would lend her opera scores she could not afford to buy herself, and throughout this period as she went about her life outside of the classroom, she would rehearse the runs, trills, roulades and cadenzas that bel canto demanded. Throughout her career she referred to the voice that was developing under de Hidalgo as though it were a separate entity. She would treat it as if it were an occasionally hostile being that had to be dealt with, confronted and negotiated with during each performance. "The voice was answering tonight," she would say after a performance, or "the voice was not obeying tonight."

Yet it was not only singing that Maria learned from de Hidalgo. She learned how to dress, how to walk across the street and stage, and how to make use of her hands and arms to generate a pulsing energy while standing still. The obsessive discipline and will that she had developed under Maria Trivella helped her to master these things—the traits that would eventually transform her into "La Divina." All of her hard work helped her to avoid the shadowy unhappiness she felt in her home life, where Evangelia lavished unconditional love and attention on Jackie while Maria felt she had to "succeed"—or at least perform—to get the same.

War and the Tigress

By 1940, Greece was readying for war and, by November, the Italians had invaded only to be beaten back into Albania. The country was celebrating when Maria made her professional debut at the National Lyric Theater, singing and dancing in Franz von Suppé's operetta, *Boccaccio*. Although she didn't perform the diva

Maria and other student performers in Suppé's Boccaccio at the Pallàs Cinema, Athens, 1941. During the war, Maria won important friends among the Italian military with her masterful renditions of Italian arias.

role, she had a solid success. She received applause, appreciation and praise as an established singer for the first time. Although her family was in the audience, it was de Hidalgo to whom she ran after the performance for reassurance that she had been sufficiently good. Her teacher's confirmation allowed her to truly savor the moment. It was not merely a mentor's nod that Maria sought from de Hidalgo; it was much more. The seventeen-year-old Maria had not spent her time flirting and making friends like most teenagers, she had concentrated on that which gave her the comfort and sense of well being that she could not get at home or else-where. It was her art that continued to be her

solace, and the more she focused on it the less she needed from home and the less interested she was in her family.

It was not long before Germany stepped in to defend Italy against the Greeks. In 1941, the German army invaded, and before long, conquered Athens. Despite the growing distance between Maria and her family, the war worked to mend those circumstances for a short time. While their army was being defeated, Evangelia, Jackie, her fiancé and their maid, Athena, set aside family squabbles to be together on the night of the German invasion. It is interesting to note that Maria's singing brought the family together. One night she sat down and began to sing and play *"La Paloma."* She was soon joined by the rest of the family and, together, through song, they created a sense of joy and comfort. As the occupation of Athens wore on, Maria's singing also wound up saving them a good deal of trouble.

Although Athens had been taken by the Germans, there were several Italian soldiers stationed there. One of the hidden benefits of her study of bel canto with de Hidalgo is that Maria was learning a style of opera that was very well known to these soldiers. There were several occasions when, despite various German proclamations against noise in both private and public spaces, the "noise" that she made at the piano that had been dragged out onto the Kalogeropoulos bal-

In a rare appearance with fellow conservatory students, at the Greek seaside, 1943.

cony made her very important friends. Indeed, one such friend was Italian Colonel Mario Bovalti from Verona. He began visiting after hearing her singing, and would accompany Maria on the piano. As time went on he began bringing little gifts and extra rations for her and the rest of the family. His attention also probably helped her emotional state as well.

Her voice aided Maria and her family—and others as well. In the autumn of 1941, a Greek officer and friend of the family showed up on their doorstep with two disguised British officers. The men had escaped from prison and needed a place to hide until the Underground could secretly convey them out of the country. At her daughter's prodding and pleading, despite her initial reluctance, Evangelia agreed to let them stay. Hidden in a small side room where the canaries were kept, the Brits were warned not to leave or make noise or to use a light after sundown. Each night, however, at nine o'clock, Maria would go to the piano and begin playing. She would sing anything that came into her head, making "noise" so that their two guests could secretly listen to the BBC from London. So well kept was this secret that not even Jackie's fiancé knew that these two men were hidden there.

After six weeks, the Greek who had brought the two officers arrived unannounced and without any explanation took them away. Despite his care, he was obviously only a few steps ahead of the authorities because, the next day, a squad of Italian soldiers pushed through their doors with weapons drawn, to search the house. Maria knew that the escaped soldiers had left letters and photos behind, but her fast thinking and natural talents saved the day. She went to the piano and began singing an aria from *Tosca*. They all came and sat around the piano, putting down their weapons and reveling in the sound of their distant homeland. The family was saved, and although the soldiers returned the next day, this time they brought loaves of bread, salamis and macaroni in appreciation of Maria's performance.

It seems likely that the soldiers she was charming were not only responding to the music of their homeland, but to a voice and a talent that were beginning to come into their own. In early summer of 1942, the aria from *Tosca* that she had used to such great effect to protect her family would offer her an opportunity to take the stage as a professional. *Boccaccio* had provided her professional stage debut, but she was young and had not had many opportunities to perform. In fact, there was a group at the Athens Opera that was resistant to Maria's being given a permanent appointment. The elderly soprano who led this party was scheduled to perform the role of Tosca, but was unable to because of ill health. Maria was suggested. The soprano fiercely opposed Maria, but too weak to stop her herself, she sent her husband to block Maria's entrance.

If the intensity of Maria's study was a result of the alienation she felt from the world and her family, it is no surprise that the anger that it masked might take little to break through. Throughout her career this fierceness would appear and eventually, besides "La Divina," Maria would gain nicknames like "The Tigress." When her adversary's husband tried to block her from performing that evening, the tigress was unleashed. She scratched his face with her fingernails. Shocked, his face bloody, he returned the attack and landed a punch to her face. With the help of some extra make-up and a hat with a wide brim, the bruise under one eye was mostly hidden, and Maria went on to astound the critics and the audience. This performance made her famous throughout Athens and cemented her place at the Athens Opera. Her natural fierceness gave a depth and drama to her Tosca, and as they would

throughout her career, her enemies, whether real or imagined, inspired the electrifying performances for which she became known.

Fame in Greece

The following summer, Maria would appear in *Tosca* not as a stand-in but as the announced star. Through her daughter's success, Evangelia was finally beginning to attain the fame that she had always wanted. Before long, people were walking ten miles from Pireaeus to hear Maria. Within the company, Evangelia became known as Maria's "Shadow," and was constantly in the dressing room ready to fan, dress and undress

"I remember the winter of 1941...Greece was invaded by the Germans and the people had already been starving for many months. We were rehearsing Tiefland and had to perform in the semi-darkness, barely lit by acetylene lamps for fear of the bombings."

—MARIA CALLAS

Maria before, after and between acts. When the Italians refused to allow Evangelia to join her daughter in northern Greece at a performance for Italian soldiers, Evangelia threatened to remove her eighteen-year-old daughter from the company. The Italians acquiesced and the two were given the royal treatment during the tour.

By 1944, Maria had begun to expand her roles. Her success as Tosca, combined with the will and focus she had developed in her studies, gave her the confidence she needed to conquer other roles. As she said in 1961, "When you are very young and on the threshold of a career you have all the confidence in the world. There is nothing you feel you couldn't tackle and do splendidly." She took on the role of Marta

Maria performing Puccini's Tosca, *at the Piazza Klathmonos Theater, Athens, 1942.*

Maria with some Italian soldiers during the war.

in Eugen d'Albert's *Tiefland* and, working intensely with conductor Leonidas Zoras through the extra rehearsals she'd demanded, she won her first standing ovation as well as international publicity on opening night. *Tiefland* had been chosen as a reaction to German complaints that the Greeks were too fond of Italian opera. Widely covered by the German-language press, she became "Maria Kalogeropoulos, Greece's foremost and most beloved opera singer."

By the end of the Axis occupation of Greece late in 1944, Maria had performed in the only modern opera she would ever appear in, *O Protomastoras* (The Masterbuilder), as well as in

Beethoven's *Fidelio* as Leonore. Her Leonore again brought the house down and cemented her place at the top of the Greek opera scene. Just before her twenty-first birthday she received from her father a letter containing a hundred dollars but with no return address. This was the first contact she had had with him in six years, and it came at a time when Maria was unsure of her next step. Although the occupation was ending and World War II was over for the

Maria as Leonore in Beethoven's Fidelio. *Reviews of the performance were universally positive, and it solidified her standing as one of Greece's foremost stars.*

Maria (back, center) with the chorus of Fidelio, *Greece, 1944.*

Greeks, fighting broke out between Communist and anti-Communist forces just a few days after her birthday. The bloody civil war had cost the family Evangelia's youngest brother. Maria was at a crossroads in her career and she wanted to escape war-wracked Greece, her controlling mother, the sister she was jealous of and her resentful colleagues at the Athens Opera.

Return to America

It is difficult to leave the comfort of home, even when it is the cause of so much personal pain. The fact that the Athens Opera refused to renew her contract helped. During this period politics played a significant role in appointments and dismissals throughout Greece, and those without overt political commitment were singled out. The company announced its refusal by saying, "She has played too active a part in the last months of the occupation." Her singing for Italian and German soldiers, her taking part in *Tiefland*, the touring she had done and the gifts of food she had accepted from the occupiers worked against her. Despite her consistent refusal to follow the petty rules of the Germans and her family's hiding of British officers, she had not done enough. But the unspoken truth was, she was never well liked at the Athens Opera, and the fame that her performances brought her certainly inspired a good deal of jealousy.

While this might have seemed like a setback it was actually just the excuse Maria was looking for. She turned to Elvira de Hidalgo for advice and her mentor insisted that she consider going to Italy. De Hidalgo had long told her that Italy was the place that she would find her audience, and, given the positive reactions of Italian soldiers stationed in Greece during the war, it is not difficult to see the wisdom behind this advice. But despite the loyalty and devotion she had for de Hidalgo, she decided to return to America. It is likely that at twenty-one the idea of being near her father—who might be seen as the "other" side in her family's battles—and therefore not completely on her own, influenced her decision. She did not

Maria with her mother and two friends on deck, 1944. On the back of the photo, her mother inscribed, "To my golden little Maria from your mommy."

bother to tell Evangelia of her plans until April 1945. She asked her mother and Jackie not to attend the September dinner that was to be given in her honor by the Mayor of Piraeus, and furthermore, requested that they not see her off at the quay. Maria was now an adult and Evangelia, doubtless in shock, did little to resist.

Maria must have been frightened returning to New York City after so long, unsure where to find her father and with only $100 in her purse. Before she left Athens, she had given her first solo concert to raise money for the trip; knowing that she had managed to leave there with some status and a sense of self-esteem must have helped, but New York can make anyone feel insignificant. As she was leaving customs, she was approached by a man she barely recognized, who asked her if she knew a Maria Kalogeropoulos. Maria fell into the arms of her father! He had learned that she was returning when he had stumbled across her name listed in a Greek-language newspaper as among the passengers bound for New York on the S.S. *Stockholm*.

Maria moved into her father's West 157th Street apartment. After the last six years of war New York seemed amazing. Just as she had when she initially arrived in Greece, she spent her first several days in America floating through the new atmosphere. Her godfather, Dr. Lantzounis, was the first person she visited. He had married an American girl, Sally, who was Maria's age, and the two of them got on famously. The doctor sent Sally out with Maria to buy some

decent clothes, and over the next days Maria spent hours wandering around New York—with Sally or her father, or by herself, often stopping to eat. Years of scarcity had only increased Maria's long-held affection for food, which was so readily available here.

Meanwhile, her father and godfather, though neither of them had much interest in or knowledge of opera, were full of encouragement, but after so many years of focus, persistence, and fierce resolve, it took her some time to return to her work. She spent her time decorating her new bedroom and keeping house and cooking for her father. It did not, however, take more than a few months before her fire for music was rekindled. By Christmas she was making the rounds of agents, studios, directors, impresarios, and her peers, but the results were something less than she had hoped. Despite the fact that she could say she had sung *Tosca, Fidelio, Tiefland* and *Cavalleria rusticana*, no one seemed particularly impressed by the stardom she had gained in Greece. Nobody knew of her fame there. When she met with the great tenor Giovanni Martinelli, who had been performing at the Met for decades, he told her that she had a good voice but she needed lessons. Such exchanges were difficult. After all, she had been a success at the Athens Opera, and now she was being told by a major player that she was not yet done with her schooling.

These rejections made her resolve even stronger. At the beginning of 1946 she was prepared to take on her critics and competitors and returned to her strenuous vocal practice. She soon met Eddie Bagarozy and his wife, Louise Caselotti. He was a lawyer who had long dabbled in opera, and Louise was a mezzo-soprano who was better known for her Hollywood musical roles than her operatic ones. Nevertheless, she was considered a very good singing teacher. Maria auditioned, and they immediately saw her great potential. This couple also liked her, and with them she could talk about opera in a way that she never could in her father's home. Already, Maria was growing tired of living with him, and was as alienated by his lack of interest and understanding of her art, as she had been by her domineering mother. The Bagarozys' Riverside Drive apartment became a second home for her

Arriving in the early morning, she would spend most of the day at the Bagarozys' apartment. She would often have dinner with them. Within this little circle, Maria began to rebuild the self-confidence that had been so badly ravaged during her first months in New York. When she was finally contacted by Edward Johnson, the general manager of the Metropolitan Opera, she was as ready for the opportunity as she had been in a long time. Immediately after her audition, she was offered a contract for leading roles in upcoming productions of *Fidelio* and *Madama Butterfly*. Much to everyone's surprise, the twenty-two-year-old newcomer turned these opportunities down. Wisely, she chose not to make her debut at the Met singing Leonore's role in English, a language she had never sung in; nor

did she wish to attempt to convince an audience that her 180-pound frame was the body of a delicately built, fifteen-year-old Japanese girl.

Given the frustrations she had experienced over the months leading up to this moment it is doubly impressive that the young Maria was so secure in her instincts. Most people did not understand her thinking. Eddie Bagarozy took the next day off from work and spent it trying to reason with her. Her mother sent her a letter as soon as she heard this news saying, "Have I suffered all these years for you so that you can go and throw away such a golden chance?" Maria's response was telling: "I'm sure I'm right. My voices have told me so." She had begun to refer to her instincts as her "voices," and both her resolve and trust in them were concrete.

The Family Reunites

Not long afterwards she auditioned for Gaetano Merola, the impresario of the San Francisco Opera. Afterwards he said, "You are young, Maria. Go and make your career in Italy and then I'll sign you up." "Thank you," she replied, "but once I have made my career in Italy I will no longer need you." This steely resolve could not last, however, and the consternation and disbelief she met with from everyone who learned of her decision began to erode her self-assurance. Maria was always her own harshest critic, but now, with her father's continuing lack of

"After the war, an enormous revolution took place in opera because of two people: Wieland Wagner, who totally changed the approach and emphasis of the physical aspects of stage direction, and Maria Callas, who took her talent almost to the point of masochism to serve her work and find its meaning."

—JON VICKERS

Maria just after her return to New York in 1945.

interest in her work and art, she found herself missing her mother. At the end of 1946, she wrote Evangelia and begged her to come to America. She was suddenly convinced that only with her mother's assistance could she achieve the promise of her future.

George, however, was less than enthusiastic about his wife's return. His modest salary from the pharmacy where he was employed meant that he would have had to make significant sacrifices to save the money required for Evangelia's trip. Maria turned to her godfather, who was willing to lend her the money. On Christmas Eve, Evangelia arrived in New York on the *Queen Elizabeth*. Maria and George met her on the docks; it was Maria who was more excited. The apathy that George had shown for anything outside his own work, combined with a provincial narrowness, had long ago alienated Evangelia from him, and they worked to do the same with his youngest daughter. Her mother's ambition was at least in line with her own mindset, and she desperately needed the "push" her mother would give her.

Despite the fact that it was the first holiday season that the three of them had spent together in nine years, it was something less than festive in the Callas household. While his family was away, George had met Alexandra Papajohn and started a steady relationship with her. Evangelia would end up sharing Maria's room from her first night there, and she took on the role of the wronged woman, who had sacrificed years of her life for her daughters while her good-for-nothing husband led a bachelor's life. This did not make for the home life that Maria had hoped for, but it did give her a close collaborator in her effort to build a career.

Lofty Ambitions

While Maria was rebuilding her "support team," Eddie Bagarozy had joined with Ottavio Scotto, an Italian agent, to launch a hugely ambitious project. They intended to revive opera in Chica-go, where the art had largely become dormant. They would do so by forming a new troupe, the United States Opera Company, to feature the best European singers. It was to be a showcase for post-World War II America, the new global super power and home of the United Nations. Despite his limited resources, Eddie used his personality and flair to assemble in New York some of the finest European talent: Max Lorenz, one of the greatest Wagnerian tenors of the time; Hilde and Anny Konetzni from Vienna; bass Nicola Rossi-Lemeni; and conductor Sergio Failoni were to be the core of the new company. They rehearsed in the Bagarozys' three-room apartment for lack of a hall.

Eddie had managed to convince the American musical world that, not only would his plans come to fruition, the result would be magical. Chicago newspapers were full of excitement about the forthcoming operatic event, *Turandot*. Puccini's last opera had not been performed in America in twenty years, and this, coupled with craftily fed rumors of the mysterious Greek who would appear in the title role, built a heady excitement. Maria, meanwhile, was thrilled by the opportunity that this would provide. Everyone involved was confident that she, at the age of 23, would manage to capture the coldness and cruelty of the Chinese princess she would play as well as the fire and sensuality roiling beneath the character's façade.

Unfortunately, an increasingly cruel fate kept the public from seeing Maria for themselves. The American Chorus Singers' Union demanded a deposit to guarantee payment to its members. Bagarozy could not meet this demand no matter how hard he worked to raise the money. The January 6th opening date was postponed for a week, then again, until finally it was set for January 27th. Eddie found the union much more difficult to charm than the press, and his momentum began to falter. He eventually declared bankruptcy for himself and the company. The Chicago Opera House organized a benefit concert and Eddie sold everything from his car and Louise's jewelry to a house they had on Long Island, in an attempt to pay his debts. While this was obviously a hardship for the Bagarozys, it was devastating to Maria.

The loss of this chance hit Maria very hard. She had invested the role of Turandot with all her feelings of frustration, and having it go awry seemed like a nasty, divine message. Being near Eddie, who despite the financial drama that had unfolded still felt that he was the guardian of a precious treasure in Maria, certainly eased her stress, but *Turandot* had become the center of her life and without it she had no center.

Her resiliency, though, was impressive. The first morning back from Chicago, Maria was at the Bagarozys', going over parts with Louise. One benefit of the prior months' endeavors was the connections she had made with some very influential European performers. Nicola Rossi-Lemeni learned that Giovanni Zenatello, a famous tenor who was now the artistic director of the Verona Festival, was in the city looking for a soprano for the lead role in Ponchielli's *La Gio-*

conda. Rossi-Lemeni had already signed a contract to sing at the festival, and convinced Zenatello to hear Maria. Zenatello was actually trying to decide between well-known sopranos Zinka Milanov and Herva Nelli at the time, but when he heard Maria sing the last act aria, *"Suicidio,"* with Louise at the piano, he was thrilled. He rushed to the piano, flipped the score to the duet between Enzo and Gioconda, and, despite his seventy years, began singing it with Maria with an impressive passion. Zenatello later described the event as "not so much an audition as a revelation" and offered the role to her on the spot.

Verona, Meneghini, and Serafin

In a frenzy of excitement, Maria and Evangelia prepared for the trip to Verona. With money from her father and godfather they put together a modest but elegant trousseau with which she would conquer Europe on and off stage. That was not all Evangelia would send her daughter off with, though. She composed a thirteen-point list of advice ending, unsurprisingly, with one of the Ten Commandments: "Honor thy father and thy mother." Besides her mother's ministrations there was also Eddie Bagarozy, who presented Maria with a contract. According to it, he was to become her "sole and exclusive personal agent for a period of ten years." For this he would receive ten percent of all of her gross fees earned in opera, concerts, radio,

Maria aboard the Rossija on her return to Italy in 1947. She is accompanied by Louise Bagarozy, soprano and wife of Eddie Bagarozy, whom Maria had reluctantly engaged as her manager before leaving the United States.

recordings and television. Bagarozy agreed in return "to use his best efforts to further and promote the Artist's career." Despite everything that he had done for her, Maria found it very difficult to sign the contract, but she ignored her "voices" and signed it on June 13th, 1947, the day she boarded the S.S. *Rossija* for Italy.

After an exhausting trip, certainly made more so by the excitement and trepidation building inside of her, Maria found herself in Verona. On her first night there, she was taken to dinner by an impressive group representing the city and the festival organizers. Among the friendly faces were some actual friends but, even with Nicola Rossi-Lemeni on hand, Maria spent the dinner mostly in silence, not unfriendly, but dutiful. That she was treated with the deference due an artist only seemed to heighten her discomfort, for it increased the pressure she felt. Zenatello had arrived in Verona before her and had made the rounds, describing with drama and enthusiasm Maria's audition in New York. Among the patrons at the dinner was a short, wiry industrialist in his early fifties, Giovanni Battista Meneghini, who was known in Verona as something of a Romeo. He was a provincial businessman whose family business had grown in the post-war years and who had acquired an air of culture through his patronage of the arts.

Meneghini was the official escort for the visiting prima donna and, good businessman and debonair man-about-town that he was, he recognized in this young woman not only talent but an important role in his future. He treated her with the sort of regard and respect that she had always wanted. Maria, who had not much experience with romance after years of pursuing little else besides her art, was completely taken by him. She would later say, "I knew he was it five minutes after I first met him." In the days following her arrival, he showed her the city and the surrounding countryside, and did so with a romantic flourish that was quite new to her. They spent a week together seeing the sights and shopping. This was also her first experience with spending money freely. Meneghini, not a particularly attractive fellow, used his wealth to enhance his charms, and Maria became a first-class shopper. Even when spending someone else's money, she loved to banter with shopkeepers whose prices were more than she

Maria with some colleagues from the Verona Arena, where she made her Italian debut in La Gioconda.

thought they should be. Throughout the rest of her life she would take great pleasure in finding knickknacks at "good" prices.

In early July rehearsals began with conductor Tullio Serafin. Thus began the Serafin period of Maria's life, and with it her advance to true diva status. As evidence of his importance to her career, she said, "He taught me that in everything there must be an expression, there must be a justification, he taught me exactly the depth of music.... I really, really drank all I could from this man." In this relationship there was a healthy give and take, as Serafin himself saw in Maria a huge talent: "As soon as I heard her sing I recognized an exceptional voice. A few notes were still uncertainly placed but I immediately knew that here was a future great singer." As any good mentor would do, he encouraged her, and she responded in rehearsal. As the opening night neared, she listened, learned and was fortified by his regard.

At the same time, Meneghini was beginning to play a vital supporting role. He was more than her escort and sugar daddy, and Maria came to trust his devotion. She found she could take his critiques of her performances more easily than she could most. The constructive criticism she received from Meneghini, combined with the inspiration from Serafin, helped her face this most important opening with surprising ease. Of course, facing 25,000 Italians, all of whom considered themselves opera critics, was still daunting. She wrote to her mother that she was "trembling like a leaf,"

even more so after a dress rehearsal when she fell on the Arena's rocky stage during an expansive moment. Meneghini dutifully spent the evening in her hotel room nursing her back to health. His calming and supportive words helped rebuild her confidence and made her feel more like a diva than a clumsy student. It may have been this event that sealed their relationship. As Maria said later, "This was just one little episode that revealed my husband's character. I would give my life for him immediately and joyfully.... If Battista had wanted, I would have abandoned my career without regret, because in a woman's life love is more important than artistic triumphs."

Despite the passion in these words, Maria might well have been over-dramatizing things—Meneghini's attentions were just what Maria needed at the time. When opening night came, she took the stage and managed to disguise the bruises and scrapes from her fall. Although the critics loved "the vibrant quality and easy production of her high notes," she did not make the splash she was hoping for. She played five more performances but the festival did not extend an invitation for the following year.

While this might have been crushing, her months in Verona were not without profit. Besides gaining a sponsor of great devotion in Meneghini, her association with Serafin was to be vital to her future. She had more resources of every type than she had ever had before. She had come a long way from rejecting the Met's contract a year earlier.

"Something New"

Around this time the assistant art director of La Scala, after hearing her sing, made some vague offers of a part in an upcoming production of Verdi's *Un ballo in maschera*, along with some comments about her vocal defects, but nothing came of any of his remarks. Meanwhile, none of the agents in Milan, the home of La Scala and veritable capital of opera, was interested in Maria. Her voice was unconventional and they were looking for something less interesting and more beautiful. "I was something new to listen to," Maria later said, "and they disliked anything that took them away from tradition." Interestingly, it was precisely within tradition that her voice lived. De Hidalgo had trained her in the art of bel canto, so alive in the first half of the nineteenth century, when the voice, its decorative flourishes and the weight given each word in the libretto were employed in the service of the emotions. Maria sought to do more than sing beautifully. "When you interpret a role, you have to have a thousand colors to portray happiness, joy, sorrow, fear. How can you do this with only a beautiful voice?"

In 1947, however, she was just a beginner, and the world was not yet sympathetic to her vision. Luckily, Serafin understood. While Maria sat in Milan growing more and more depressed as the rejections piled up, he sent an official from La Fenice in Venice to sign her up for the productions of *Tristan und Isolde* and *Turandot* that he would be conducting there at the end of the

"Serafin…called me to perform Isolde… I had just looked at the first act by curiosity and at the last minute he asked for an audition with me. And I wouldn't dare say I didn't know the opera, for I would have lost the audition…so I just bluffed. I said, 'Yes of course I know Isolde,' and I sight-read the second act. I don't know how. God must have helped me…and he turned around and said 'Excellent work, I must say you know the role well.' And then I confessed. 'Look, Maestro,' I said, 'I must say I bluffed'…Well, he was surprised and he appreciated me even more then."

—MARIA CALLAS

year. She signed the contract immediately and it was only afterwards that she acknowledged that she did not know Isolde. While Meneghini was supportive, it was Serafin himself who calmed her fears when she admitted to him that the role was new to her. He simply laughed and

Maria in a production of Puccini's Turandot *at La Fenice, Venice, in January of 1948. Her performance in this taxing role revealed the scope and versatility of her talent.*

assured her that she would only need a month of study to make it hers. After weeks of depression, Maria felt ready to take on the world.

As always, she did not sit back and await victory. She spent December tearing into Isolde, and it was her first triumph since Athens. Her Turandot in January 1948 made the frustrations of the past few years seem worthwhile. That this was the same role that was supposed to have made her name in America only made things sweeter. Still, not everyone "got" her and her approach. It would take more than two brilliant performances to persuade the world to listen in a different way.

Some old friends were among those who did not understand Maria's art. Louise Caselotti voiced concerns after hearing the *Turandot*: "The soaring high notes we admired when we were preparing the part for Chicago had lost their freedom and hovered badly. Her low register was also weak. I knew that she was on the wrong track and told her so." Maria took such comments as disloyalty, so it was easy for her to break off relations with the Bagarozys and pledge herself to Meneghini and Serafin, whose ministrations had gotten her where she was.

Growing Success

Maria soon began to receive offers from all over. In the next year she appeared in Venice, Udine, Trieste, Genoa, Rome, Turin, Rovigo and Florence. She had still not cracked La Scala, the Met or Covent Garden, but she built a string of performances during 1948 that would provide a firm base from which she might easily launch herself into those citadels of operatic greatness. Besides Isolde and Turandot, which she performed several times that year, she also sang her first Verdi heroine, Leonora in *La forza del destino*. This role, unlike the others, was filled with Italianate grace and expression that made use of her bel canto skills.

In June she spent the entire month working with Serafin on a character that would become

definitively hers, Bellini's Norma. In fact, during these months the two became inseparable, and Serafin gave her all of his free time. There is little doubt that this attention is what helped Maria to define Norma so completely. Throughout this whirlwind of work, Meneghini was behind the scenes. He may have begun merely as an escort, but he had become the person upon whom Maria could rely. In a strange way, he became both mother and father to her. Maria's focus on her career would not permit a broader definition of love or romance, and Meneghini was smart enough not to question things. He was, after all, little more than a great fan whose wealth permitted him access where another could only have watched from afar. He took the opportunity to become vital to Maria's rise.

Meneghini's family, did not see things the same way, however, and when the couple returned to Verona in the summer of 1948 for Maria to sing Turandot, Mama Meneghini's complaints about her son being used and manipulated by a "woman of the stage" had began to seep into the rumor mills of the provincial elite. Maria was subjected to an uncomfortable series of snubs, and was distraught at the rumors that she was only interested in Meneghini for his wealth. He was unaffected by his family's resistance, and began to focus his energies on Maria's career. He was coming to fulfill the function of personal manager, and he clearly wanted to become her husband. As much as she trusted and depended upon him, she would write to her mother, "I have met a man who is madly in love with

Maria (right) witnessing Liu's death scene in the last act of Puccini's Turandot, La Fenice, 1948.

me. He wants to marry me. I don't know what to tell him He is fifty-three; what do you think? He's very rich and he loves me." Evangelia was no more thrilled by the prospect of an older son-in-law than Meneghini's mother was of a younger daughter-in-law. Maria turned to her godfather, who had married a much younger woman. He advised her to follow her instincts—something that must have struck a chord with her—and suggested that she could be as happy with an older man as he was with a younger woman.

Winning Hearts in Italy

Despite this drama, Maria was in no hurry to make a decision and Meneghini did not push her. During a series of performances of *Aida*, she worked on Norma, and as long as her support "team" was in place she could focus. On November 30th, in Florence, she sang Norma for the first time. *Norma* is the greatest of Bellini's operas and it places as much significance on the words as it does the very-difficult music. Richard Wagner appreciated the role of Norma so much that he said, while composing *Tristan und Isolde*, that he hoped "Isolde would become [his] Norma." Maria instinctively knew the depth of this character and the role captured her imagination entirely. She told Serafin before the first performance that "It will never be as good as it is now, in my mind, unsung."

The work is probably the pinnacle of the bel canto repertoire and she knew it. The arias and recitatives were just the beginning of the score's demands. The full range of trills, scales,

Maria as Norma, her most often performed role, at La Scala, 1952.

epic breath control and ornamentation intrinsic to bel canto technique are the cornerstones of the role. And it requires great stamina—Norma is onstage and singing for three-quarters of the opera, and the most challenging music comes

in the final scene. Maria was more than ready for the virtuosity required for the role and, through almost obsessive practicing, she sharpened her technique even further to meet its challenges.

If Maria was looking to capture the heart of the Italian audience, she could not have chosen a better role. Bellini had written Norma with the knowledge that the singer and the song were supreme. At the Teatro Comunale in Florence, the young singer was compared with the great American soprano Rosa Ponselle, and, much further back, to Giuditta Pasta, for whom Bellini had written the part. With the raves of the reviewers and the accolades of the crowds ringing in her ears Maria left Florence for Venice and a Wagnerian role new to her, Brünnhilde in *Die Walküre*.

While she was preparing for *Die Walküre,* Serafin was working on Bellini's *I puritani*; he was going to conduct both of these works in Venice in early 1949. Maria spent any time she was not studying Norma in the maestro's suite at the Hotel Regina. Taking a break from the exhausting rehearsals, she discovered the score of *Puritani* and began sight-reading one of Elvira's arias. Serafin's wife was on the phone in the next room and, when she heard Maria singing, she went to see. Madame Serafin could not help but stand frozen in the doorway listening to the performance. The call she had been on had been her husband telling her that Margherita Carosio, who was one of Italy's premier sopranos, had come down with a bad flu, and would not be able to take the role of Elvira as planned. Understanding her husband's desperation as he tried to find a replacement only ten days before opening night, and amazed by what she had just heard, she asked Maria to sing the aria for him when he returned.

After doing so, Maria returned to her room for the evening and Serafin made no comment. The next morning, however, Maria's phone rang at ten and she was asked to come to the maestro's room. She protested that she was still in her robe, that it would take her thirty minutes to wash and dress. He responded, "No, no, no, come down as you are." She complied immediately and, when she entered his rooms, there was another man there. She recognized him as the opera house's musical director.

"Sing," Serafin said. Maria was confused by the command and in response he explained, "Sing what you sang to me yesterday."

Still somewhat confused and sleepy-eyed, Maria found the aria in the score and sight-read it again. She stood there awkwardly as the two men spoke in hushed tones. "Well, Maria," Serafin finally said, "you are going to do this role in a week."

She attempted to argue that she had several more *Walküres* to perform and she could not possibly take on this second role so quickly. "I guarantee that you can," he replied and her only response could be, "Maestro, my best I can do. More than my best I cannot promise." As she said in a later interview, her only thought was, "Well, if they are crazy enough to believe I can

Maria as Abigaille in Nabucco *at San Carlo di Napoli, 1949. She only performed this voice-wrecking role three times.*

do it ... I am still young, and when you are growing you have to gamble."

Much to the surprise of the opera world the gamble paid off. Opera and film director Franco Zefferelli commented after her death, "What she did in Venice was really incredible. You need to be familiar with opera to realize the size of her achievement that night. It was as if someone had asked Birgit Nilsson, who is famous for her great Wagnerian voice, to substitute overnight for Beverly Sills, who is one of the top coloratura sopranos of our time." Given the spectacular flexibility this performance showed, it is understandable that the audience was willing to forgive the minor flubs she made that night. Since she had not had time to memorize Elvira's words, she was forced to make use of a prompter, and during the aria, *"Son vergin vezzosa"* (I am a charming virgin) she misunderstood the prompter and sang *"Son vergin viziosa"* (I am a vicious virgin). In spite of all, the audience—even Carosio's fans, who had come for blood—and the press praised her to the skies.

Overnight Maria had become the toast of Italy. After so many years of hard work and intense focus she received the acceptance of the opera community. She became known as a singer among singers, and became the focal point around which the bel canto repertoire would be rehabilitated. Never one to rest on her laurels, certainly not so early in her career, Maria moved on to perform all across Italy. Along with appearances in opera houses, Radio Italiana invited her to sing a program of Verdi, Wagner and Bellini arias

in Turin, and in November she made her first commercial recording, for Cetra, of a selection of Wagner and Bellini arias.

"Married and Happy"

As her professional life continued to gain momentum throughout 1949, her personal life settled comfortably. While she was preparing for her appearance at the Teatro Colón in Buenos Aires in May, she realized that it would be the first time that she and "Titta," as she had come to call Meneghini, would be separated since they had met. Her successes combined with his stalwart support throughout the last eventful year

Maria and Battista Meneghini on April 21, 1949, just after they were married.

Maria performing the title role in Puccini's Turandot *at the Teatro Colon, Buenos Aires, in June 1949. This was the last of her 24 performances of the role.*

finally convinced her that she should marry him. After he gained a dispensation from the Catholic Church to marry outside the religion, they were married in the Chiesa dei Filippini in Verona. Besides two of Titta's friends, who acted as witnesses, and the priest and the sacristan, there was nobody else present at the simple ceremony. Just before she boarded the ship for Argentina, she sent her parents a cablegram: *"Siamo sposati e felici"* (We are married and happy). The significance of this break with her family could not be missed.

She wowed the audience of the Teatro Colon with her Turandot. "In the role of Turandot Maria Callas showed all her vocal gifts as well as her magnetic presence," wrote the critic for *La Nación.* Not all her notices were positive, but a singer who so deliberately tried to show the world something new could not be expected to be loved by everyone. Upon her return to Italy she began creating a home in the penthouse Meneghini had purchased and decorated for them.

Despite the fact that Zeffirelli later referred to the décor as " a poor man's Zsa Zsa Gabor," Maria loved her new home. She threw herself into becoming a proper Italian housewife, even picking up a Veronese accent to go along with the pasta she would spend hours preparing. She could not stay away from the stage for long,

however, and in 1950 she appeared as Norma in Venice, Aida in Brescia, Isolde in Rome, Norma in Catania, and added Tosca and *Il trovatore's* Leonora in Mexico City. With each performance her fame grew, yet there was no sign from La Scala. It was becoming worrisome—and then Milan finally called.

Soprano Renata Tebaldi's star had risen just a year before Maria's. The two women were rivals within the small world of opera, but they had attended each other's performances when possible and had been vocal in their mutual sup-

Maria in a revival of Aida *at the Palacio de Bellas Artes, Mexico, 1950.*

port. With her creamy voice, direct, uncomplicated personality and stage presence, Tebaldi was easy for Italian audiences to relate to. She had already premiered at La Scala and was held in the highest esteem by audiences, critics and her peers. Now she had fallen ill and La Scala turned to Maria to replace her as Aida.

La Scala at Last

It was too big an opportunity to pass up, but it still stung considerably not to have been offered an opera of her own. When asked whether she was excited about appearing at La Scala her reply sent a clear message: "La Scala, magnificent theater....Yes, I am thrilled, of course I am thrilled. But I am nearsighted, you see. For me all theatres are alike. Am I excited? La Scala is La Scala, but I am nearsighted: *ecco tutto*." La Scala would get Callas, but only on Callas' terms without bowing and scraping or thanks. Callas was becoming the Callas of Legend very quickly.

Regardless of her hurt feelings, Maria knew that she needed her debut at La Scala to be memorable. From there she could attain even greater heights. Between the tremendous stress she placed herself under and the frustration she felt at the nature of her debut, she did not leave the Milanese press with the best impression. For example, when asked how she felt about the public, she responded, "The public? What about the public? If I sing well they applaud, if they don't like me they whistle. It's the same

everywhere." It is no surprise, then, that the critical reaction to her Aida was lukewarm. The audience, which was filled with ministers, foreign dignitaries, even the president of Italy himself, was polite—but the offer of a permanent engagement from La Scala was not forthcoming.

Besides her own lack of diplomacy, Maria was faced with an even greater obstacle at La Scala: the legendary opera house's manager, Antonio Ghiringhelli. He was known to prefer stars that he could control, and in Maria he saw a woman that he could not easily categorize or manipulate. With Ghiringhelli standing in her way, she finished her remaining *Aidas* and left for her next engagement, which was in Naples. Just as she had decided that she would play the Met on her own terms, her future dealings with La Scala were to be conducted her own way, not Ghiringhelli's.

Rivalries

The following year, Maria had several more successes before flying, via New York City, to Mexico City for her debut there. While her stop in New York was a kind of victorious homecoming, it was overshadowed by the fact that Evangelia was ill and in the hospital. Maria was glad to see her father and godfather again, but it was her mother who had most of her focus. Evangelia responded remarkably to Maria's presence. Maria invited her mother to come to Mexico City

The Palacio de Bellas Artes welcomes Maria Callas to its 1950 season. Her mother met her there, but it was the last time the two would ever see each other.

when she got out of the hospital. The result was a remarkably speedy recovery.

In Mexico City, Maria was treated with the respect and exaltation that her growing fame merited—and then some. Her performances as Norma, Aida, Tosca, and Leonora in *Il trovatore*, which was new to her repertoire, garnered rave reviews and adoring audiences. When Evangelia finally arrived, she was greeted at the airport by Mexican dignitaries and discovered her room at the Hotel Prince full of flowers. It was pre-

cisely the sort of life she had dreamed of living, and she knew that it was her early efforts that had launched Maria toward such fame. She was given, and took, a full share of her daughter's glory.

Outside of the public's view, however, things were not going well between mother and daughter. Evangelia said in a later interview that, "Maria was formally, sometimes ostentatiously kind, as she might be to a distant relative, a cousin perhaps whom she had known for years and was fond of only at arm's length." In leaving Greece and going to America Maria had attempted to free herself from Evangelia, but it was only when she finally followed de Hidalgo's advice and went to Italy that she managed to do so and to succeed on her own terms. Mexico City was an opportunity to give Evangelia her due, all the while making it clear to her that she was no longer necessary.

But this was not nearly as true as Maria would have liked. In addition to her mother's taking care of her underwear and giving her alcohol rubs when she returned exhausted after a performance, Maria needed her emotional support. Following the first performance of *Aida*, Maria retired for the evening. Evangelia could hear her sobbing. Going to investigate, she assumed that Maria was upset about the performance, but when she asked, Maria wept and told her that what she really wanted was children: "I want many children around me.... And I want you to bring them up...." She cried herself to sleep in her mother's arms. But when she woke up the next morning, and Evangelia tried to give her

Maria with her husband Battista Meneghini and fans, backstage, 1950. With Evangelia out of the picture, Meneghini became Maria's primary emotional support. He tended to fuel Maria's paranoia, thereby solidifying his position in her life.

a good-morning kiss, Maria pushed her aside saying, "Don't, Mother, I'm no longer a child!" The feelings of resentment in Maria ran very deep.

This was not the only conflict Maria found herself in while in Mexico. She had always viewed her career as a battle, and Meneghini's way of supporting her was to encourage this. Critics were either with her or against her. Her peers either stepped aside or were seen as interlopers. In Mexico, she succumbed to infighting both on and off the stage. In *Aida*, she crossed swords with Kurt Baum, who was playing Radames, just as she had during earlier performances of *Norma* in which he had played Pollione. Their animosity overflowed in front of the proscenium: During the first night's performance, Baum continually held his high notes too long, which not only irritated Maria, but enraged bass Nicola Moscona, who was singing the part of Ramfis.

Maria had originally met Moscona in Athens, but when she attempted to see him in New York he initially put her off, finally agreed to see her, but then refused to introduce her to conductor Arturo Toscanini. Because of this slight, Maria refused to have anything to do with him. Now, however, she set that aside in order to form an alliance with him against Baum. Meeting in secret, in Maria's dressing room, they developed a plan to avenge themselves. (Alternate accounts claim that the company's manager, Antonio Caraza-Campos made the suggestion of revenge, but agree that Moscona was more

than happy about it.) In the next performance, at the close of the Triumphal Scene, Maria's voice climbed an octave rather than ending as Verdi had written it, to an orchestra-riding high E-flat. She sustained the E-flat through to the end of the orchestral finale. Baum found himself challenged by a well-organized opposition (not only had Maria and Moscona developed this strategy, they had confided in their other colleagues, Giulietta Simionato and Robert Weede, who had agreed to allow the soprano to upstage Baum). As a result of Maria's amazing vocal endurance, Baum declared that he would never sing with her again. Of course, all of this was thrilling for the audience, and even the Verdi-purists had to acknowledge that the brilliant singing made up for the trespass.

"When one is a young performer, one is more of an athlete than an artist." This statement from Maria surely explains the antics of the Mexico City *Aida*. The result of all of the oversinging—both Baum's and Maria's—was an amazing performance that further established Maria's renown.

Italy and Visconti

After several more operas filled with Olympic vocal athletics, the 1950 Mexico City opera season came to a close. Maria went off to Madrid, leaving Evangelia with a new fur coat, money for her hospital bills and $700 she was instructed to give to Maria's godfather, to repay him.

If Maria was returning to Europe at the top of her game and the beginning of her fame, to a husband who doted on her, Evangelia had very different prospects before her. Her marriage was unhappier than ever, she was older and frailer, and her relationship with the daughter whom she had for so many years pushed and prodded towards fame and success was formally pleasant, but privately miserable. Maria seemed to care little, and, as it turned out, the two never saw each other again.

Titta met Maria in Madrid and they took three months off so that she could prepare for the coming year. After her triumph in Mexico, Maria believed that she might have the same success in Italy. She had finally earned some respect in Verona. Dinner invitations from fashionable Italian hostesses were the greatest proof of this newfound regard. While she had managed to conquer the stage, she still found herself awkward in social circumstances and these engagements became as much a performance as the operatic ones. Consequently, her three months off were less relaxing than they might have been, she became irritable and began to overreact to minor slights. Titta lent emotional support as always, by validating Maria's moods. If nothing else, as long as there was an enemy, his role as protector was set and his position secure, so he permitted Maria's anxieties to feed on themselves. Thus a difficult diva was born.

One of Maria's final operas of 1950, *Il turco in Italia*, was not only her first role in a comic opera, but, more importantly, it was her first

with director Luchino Visconti. Visconti would take over from Serafin in Maria's professional life, and unlike earlier mentors the two would become utterly infatuated with each other. He was Italy's best known film director at the time and he had an air of aristocratic distinction that she could not resist. And Visconti had been drawn to Maria after seeing her the previous year in Rome in *Parsifal*. The role in *Il turco* was new for her, and the context in which the opera was chosen was new as well. Visconti was a member of the Anfiparnasso group, a coalition of left-wing artists and intellectuals. Although their politics held little interest for Maria, she enjoyed the discussions of revolution, new art and new morals, particularly as they were filtered through Visconti himself. It is easy to see how this group came upon the idea of reviving an opera in which a flighty young wife of an old Neapolitan nobleman falls madly in love with a faithless Turkish sultan and sings about the joys of infidelity. Given the comparative lightness of the role, Maria's success in it again underlined her amazing artistic flexibility. "Maria Callas was the surprise of the evening," wrote Opera's Roman correspondent after the opening night of *Il turco*. "She sang a light soprano role with the utmost ease, making it extremely difficult to believe that she can be the perfect interpreter of both Turandot and Isolde."

This artistic flexibility may have put her in the spotlight, but it also cost her a good deal. After returning from Mexico to a stressful social life in Verona, and then following that with *Il turco* and several other roles around Italy, Maria's body was pushed to its limit. During rehearsals for *Don Carlo* she caught a case of jaundice and her doctor ordered complete rest and the cancellation of all performances in Naples and Rome.

During this time, Maria learned that Evangelia had returned to Greece to be with Jackie, and that she was extremely unhappy with George. Evangelia wrote to Maria, reminding her of her vital role in helping Maria achieve fame—and she sked for money. That Titta was a millionaire and Maria was quite well paid only made it seem more unjust to Evangelia that her daughter was not being financially forthcoming. Maria's responses to these letters were scant, and Evangelia began to focus her anger on the person who had taken her place at Maria's side: Meneghini. This, of course, only drove her daughter

Maria and Meneghini visiting Maria's father, George Kalogeropoulous, in New York.

further away. In what might be interpreted as a result of the dramatic decline in her relationship with Evangelia, Maria invited George to join her in Mexico in the summer of 1951. If there was a peculiar distance between Maria and Evangelia when they parted in Mexico City, their relationship was now utterly poisoned.

As she was recovering from jaundice and carrying on a war of words with her mother, Italy was celebrating the fiftieth anniversary of Verdi's death. In Florence in January 1951, Maria worked with Serafin for the first time since Mexico City. It was her first *Traviata,* and she had been working on it for two years, since she'd gone to Buenos Aires for the first time with Serafin. She had gained a good deal of self-confidence and was not nearly as submissive toward the maestro as she had once been. The two had their first falling out during rehearsals for *Traviata,* but on opening night those feelings could not be detected. In front of the curtain after the end of the performance they stood before an adoring audience hand in hand, and Serafin said, "Here was a great accomplishment, and it surprised many."

While Maria continued to surprise audiences and critics, not everyone was convinced. To Maria and her supporters the surprise was that anyone could fail to see the depth of her talent. It is notable that while she was not new to infighting and quarrels with her peers on stage and off, she could also inspire a good deal of affection. When the Naples media did not respond glowingly to her first *Trovatore* in Italy at the end of January 1951, Giacomo Lauri-Volpi, who sang Manrico in the performance, wrote a letter to the Neapolitan press decrying "this dreadful indifference" to Maria's greatness.

Conquering La Scala and Battling Tebaldi

A panicked call she received from La Scala not long after she left Naples received an icy reply. Ghiringhelli once again found himself needing to replace an indisposed Renata Tebaldi. Maria's refusal made it clear that she would not return to La Scala until Ghiringhelli was willing to acknowledge that she merited, indeed, was owed, a proper debut. The message was not lost on the authoritarian Ghiringhelli, but when director Gian Carlo Menotti told him that he wanted Maria for the role of Magda in *The Consul,* the manager of La Scala's reaction was, "Oh, my god! No, never, never, never! I promised you than any singer you chose would be acceptable to me, but I will not have Maria Callas in the theatre unless she comes as a guest artist."

Ghiringelli was wrong. At the end of May, Maria's performance as Elena in *I vespri siciliani* in Florence was such a popular and critical success that La Scala could no longer hold out. La Scala offered her three leading roles, thirty appearances during her initial season, at nearly $500 a performance (a very handsome sum

in 1951). The financial arrangement, however, was inconsequential compared to the significance of the capital of opera's impassioned (desperate?) invitation. Crowned with this glory Maria landed in Mexico City with Titta and met her father, who was waiting for them. While he had never really understood her love of opera, would have cancelled her music lessons completely during the early 1930s and had mocked her attempts a few years earlier to get the Met's attention when she returned to New York, George certainly appreciated the exaltation his daughter received now. It also helped that he got along with Meneghini famously. Now that she was older and successful George was no longer distant and disinterested. Perhaps most importantly, his interest was unencumbered by the demands and expectation that came with Evangelia's. Throughout this time with her father, Maria relished having him in the audience, and her love for him grew even as her resentment toward her mother increased.

Once again Maria left Mexico with an unmitigated triumph behind her. By the time she arrived in São Paulo, Brazil, for the next leg of her South American tour, she was physically exhausted. Her doctor made her cancel all of her performances of Aida there, and she only appeared in *Traviata.* In this opera she traded performances as Violetta with Tebaldi. Given the nature of the personalities involved, it is not much of a surprise that the divas found sharing the limelight difficult. Maria had already received

Maria in La Traviata *during her second Mexican season, 1951.*

"If the time comes when my dear friend Renata Tebaldi sings Norma *or* Lucia *one night, then* Violetta, La Gioconda, *or* Medea *the next — then and only then will we be rivals. Otherwise it is like comparing Champagne with Cognac. No — with Coca-Cola."*

—MARIA CALLAS

her first bad press from South American critics for cancelling her Aidas, and it might be said that this was the beginning of the press's revelry in Maria's rivalries.

Things fell apart onstage between the two sopranos at a benefit concert in Rio de Janeiro. When Maria arrived in the city she immediately heard about Tebaldi's success as Violetta. Maria received equal praise for her Norma soon after, and the stage was set for a dramatic clash between the two. What made this rivalry unique was the role the public played in it. The opera world split into two factions: Tebaldists and Callasites. These groups supported their prima donnas with impressive adoration, which incited Tebaldi and Callas to even greater competition. At

Renata Tebaldi, 1950.
Tebaldi and Callas had equally adoring fans, which
certainly exacerbated their rivalry.

the benefit concert, Maria sang *"Sempre libera"* from *Traviata,* while Tebaldi sang the "Ave Maria" from *Otello.* Maria's performance was excellent and after her curtain calls she withdrew; Tebaldi, also sang beautifully and gave two encores. This was despite an agreement not to give encores, and Maria took her rival's action very badly. It seemed to her that Tebaldi had purposely sought to outdo her. There were ugly words exchanged and the two camps broke off diplomatic relations.

Throughout the days that followed the two divas were constantly within reach of each other. Not only were they splitting performances in *Traviata,* they were invited to the same social functions. In what was surely the low point in their fractious relationship, an after-dinner conversation between the two nearly turned into a brawl. If this seems ludicrous, the repercussions of these fights were all too serious. After Maria's opening night performance of *Tosca,* Meneghini rushed into her dressing room reporting rumors of an anti-Callas plan. Granted, this was not unusual on Titta's part, but not long after, she was asked to come to the office of Barreto Pinto, the director of the opera house. When she arrived Pinto told her that because of extremely unfavorable audience reactions to her performance, her contract was terminated. Maria managed to keep her head and reminded him that due to contractual obligations he would have to pay her for the second *Tosca* and two *Traviatas* that he was canceling. This enraged Pinto, but he had no choice in the matter. Her replacement was, of course, Tebaldi, and Maria publicly accused her of influencing Pinto's decision. That there was no proof of this was irrelevant to the Callasites. When Maria went to collect the fees she was owed, Pinto, who hated her by this point, could not help but taunt her. "So you want money on top of glory, eh?" he said, and Maria finally lost what control she had and picked up an inkstand from his desk to throw at him. His secretary sprang forward and grabbed it from her. When the press got hold of this story she was painted as every bit as vicious and difficult as some of the characters she portrayed. But she still had much of South America's sympathy, and when she returned to Italy she had to attempt to put the tribulations behind her and prepare for La Scala.

Milan Surrenders to Maria

In Milan, Ghiringhelli was determined that La Scala's *I vespri siciliani* would outshine the memory of the prior summer's brilliant production in Florence. As one would expect from Italy's premier opera house, the best talent was collected and there was ample rehearsal time. Maria dove in and stunned everyone with the range that was becoming her hallmark. As one member of the chorus later recalled, "she came onstage sounding like our deepest contralto, Cloe Elmo. Before the evening was over, she took a high E-flat, and it was twice as strong as Toti dal Monte's!" [a famous coloratura soprano] Maria's professionalism and commitment, combined

Maria in I vespri Siciliani *at La Scala, 1951. Tebaldi later claimed that Maria's arrival at La Scala left no room for her.*

with her vocal flexibility, put her in good stead with her peers, but the opening night audience was cautious in its expectations. This was, after all, the city in which even garbage men considered themselves experts on opera, and even if the audience could not sing the arias themselves, they could, and would, certainly whistle anyone off stage who could not do so to their expectations.

Maria knew that if she could conquer La Scala, her fame would be validated. The Met, Covent Garden, and every other grand opera house in the world would open themselves to her, and the history books would never forget her name. Throughout her career she would report that before every performance the terror she felt was intense. It is to her credit, and a sign of her character and talent, that she managed to overcome her fears and quell the beast that La Scala's audience could become. Their surrender was total, and the applause at the end of the Bolero, *"Mercè, dilette amiche,"* which opened the last act, let her know that she had earned the respect of Milan. The critics agreed: "The miraculous throat of Maria Meneghini Callas ... the prodigious extension of her tones, their phosphorescent beauty and her technical agility which is more than rare, it is unique." *(Corriere della Sera)*

The opera world was ready for somebody unique, that is, somebody who could shake things up and revivify the art form. The next few years were full of corresponding victories: She was signed to a recording contract at EMI by producer Walter Legge, who would be a vital

Maria at La Scala in 1954, with EMI producer Walter Legge and conductor Victor de Sabata, discussing a recording.

influence on her throughout her career; she gave several brilliant performances and premiered at Covent Garden in *Norma,* beginning a love affair with the English that would last throughout her career; and, perhaps most dramatically, by the end of 1954 she had lost close to seventy pounds.

Maria Takes Off

Maria's weight had been an issue since her childhood. Indeed, one of the reasons that she had turned down the Met's initial offer was that she could hardly be convincing in the role of Butterfly due to her bulk. The reviewers had never been kind about it either; as one in Verona wrote after her first appearance in *Aida,* "it was impossible to tell the difference between the legs of the elephants on the stage and those of Aida sung by Maria Callas." Needless to say, Maria was desperately hurt by such remarks. Besides the social embarrassment that her weight caused, the physical effort of bearing it was a major issue. By 1954, she was bothered by headaches, fainting spells and attacks of car sickness that she blamed on her weight. The impressive thing about her weight-loss was that she told nobody she was planning it. With the amazing willpower that she had cultivated throughout her life and that had enabled her to become the star that she was, she put her mind to losing the weight and did so.

While she was slimming down from hefty to Audrey Hepburn-like, Maria was dominating the stage as few of her contemporaries, regardless of their faction's claims, could.

Throughout her career, from her earliest days with de Hidalgo, Maria sought roles that called for dramatic as well as vocal intensity. In 1953, she once again opened La Scala's season, this time as Lady Macbeth. Not only was this to be the first televised opera performance, but it was the first time Maria appeared in the part. It was a role, along with Norma and Medea, that she would define and that would come to define her. Just as central to her, and she to it, was Lucia di Lammermoor, which she interpreted in a new and exciting way.

Maria as Lady Macbeth at La Scala in 1952. Shortly after the 1952 season, Maria quietly began her weight-loss program, eventually losing more than eighty pounds.

Maria with Herbert von Karajan and members of the chorus, after her triumphant performance in Donizetti's Lucia di Lammermoor, *1954.*

Maria consults with conductor Herbert von Karajan during a 1954 dress rehearsal of Lucia *at La Scala. Callas is credited with restoring a sense of dramatic urgency which had been all but stripped from the role by light-voiced, coloratura songbird-sopranos.*

Despite the successes of her early Lucias, it was for conductor Herbert von Karajan at La Scala that she brought out the terror of the Mad Scene in a way nobody in recent memory had. Rather than sing it as a light, flute-imitation-crazy showpiece, as most sopranos did, Maria realized the raw emotional intensity of the moments following Lucia's murder of the husband she had been forced to marry. She scared and spellbound the audiences and caused a musical revolution; the role was hers.

Medea, meanwhile, was the part in which the new, slimmed-down Maria made her debut. When she was heavy, she did not feel as if she could play the part of the lean, fierce Medea: "...I was tired of playing a game like—for instance—playing a beautiful young woman, and I was a heavy, uncomfortable woman finding it difficult to move around..." Not only that, but as she said, "... the face is too fat and I can't stand it, because I needed the chin for expression in certain very hard phrases, cruel phrases

Medea at La Scala, 1953. It was the first performance of the opera in Italy in over 45 years.

"My Wife Will Not Sing at the Met"

By the time she portrayed Medea at the Teatro Comunale in Florence, Maria had not only transformed herself physically but had established herself as an artist who was changing opera. But there were still stages to conquer. She had yet to appear at the Metropolitan Opera, and she and Titta were very aware of this. The Met's general manager, Rudolf Bing, was in the audience at the Teatro Comunale and afterwards he approached Maria and made very clear his interest in having her grace his stage at the earliest opportunity. Meneghini, after many years of running Maria's business, was like a cat playing with a trapped mouse. It was in his nature to play hard-to-get in these situations, and he made financial demands that Bing could barely consider. The talks went on for some time, but finally Meneghini angrily told the press that, "My wife will not sing at the Metropolitan as long as Mr. Bing runs it. It is their loss."

While relations between the Callas-Meneghinis and the Met broke down, other relationships seemed to be on the mend—or were they? Wally Toscanini, Arturo Toscanini's daughter, had become very close to Maria and had long been attempting to replace Renata Tebaldi with Maria in her father's circle. Alfredo Catalani's *La Wally*, for which Toscanini had named his daughter, was to open the 1953-54 La Scala season to honor the sixtieth anniversary of the composer's death. Tebaldi was chosen by Toscanini for

or tense phrases. And I felt—as the woman of theater that I was and am—that I needed these necklines and the chinlines to be very thin and very pronounced." Just as she had brought out the primal terror in Lucia's Mad Scene, Callas would alter the audience's perception of Medea. The role had not been performed in Italy in 45 years and through her physical presence and vocal performance she brought out the raw primitivism, flaming jealousy, and visceral hatred that had been masked and dulled by the classical tradition in which it was steeped.

the role and the factions were lining up for what promised to be a rather operatic, clash. Ghiringhelli had split the season equally between the two divas with Callas getting *Lucia, Don Carlo, Alceste* and *Medea;* Tebaldi would have *Otello, Tosca* and *Eugene Onegin* as well as *La Wally.* Since Maria had opened the season the

Wanda Toscanini with her husband, the celebrated pianist Vladimir Horowitz. Wanda was instrumental in securing a place for Maria in her father's inner circle.

Arturo Toscanini conducting at La Scala.

year before he gave Renata the honor of opening this year. Regardless of their rivalry, and doubtless to the chagrin of their more active fans, Maria was present on opening night, cheering on her rival. When Maria opened *Medea* a few nights later Tebaldi failed to return the compliment and did not appear; nor did Toscanini, who had certainly been in the house for Tebaldi's opening night.

Before *Medea* opened, Tebaldi was the least of Maria's concerns. Originally, Scarlatti's *Mitridate Eupatore* was scheduled, but after the spectacular premiere in Florence, Ghiringhelli had to bring *Medea* to Milan. This last minute change was a nightmare for director Margherita Wallman, who not only had to deal with the costume and set changes, but just ten days before opening night, Victor de Sabata fell ill, leaving

*Maria and Leonard
Bernstein hit it off
famously when
Bernstein was called in
to replace an indisposed
Victor de Sabata as
conductor of Cherubini's
Medea at La Scala,
1954.*

La Scala without a conductor. Luckily, Leonard Bernstein was just ending a tour of Italy. Actually, it might not have seemed so lucky at first because, despite the fact that the thirty-five year old conductor had written musicals and a symphony, directed the New York Philharmonic and taught at Brandeis University, he had never conducted opera. Ghiringhelli did not see this as a problem, though, and sent him the score, which was entirely new to Bernstein. It did not take long for him to fall in love with Cherubini's work and, despite the fact that he was fighting off an acute case of bronchitis, he accepted the job.

Along with the exhaustion he felt having just ended his long tour and illness, he had two specific problems directly related to the opera. One was how to deal with a very old, dusty, tattered score; the other, which a much greater challenge, was that he wanted to cut one of Medea's arias. As it turned out, the relative challenge of these two matters was quite different than he expected. While the first problem inflamed his bronchial passages, he found working with the diva with the ferocious reputation more than made up for it. He would later say, "To my absolute amazement she understood immediately the dramatic reasons for the transposition of scenes and numbers, and the cutting out of her aria in the second act. We got along famously—just perfect. She understood everything I wanted and I understood everything she wanted." Her years of study gave her a deep understanding of the music and drama, which is clearly not what Bernstein had expected from a diva. For her part, Maria found the conductor to be charming, witty and possessing a

Bernstein and Callas pause for a press photo after a triumphant performance of Medea *at* La Scala, *1954. Each had great respect for the other's dramatic sense.*

Maria with bass Nicola Rossi-Lemeni in a Chicago Lyric Opera performance of Norma. *Acting as Maria's manager, Meneghini would not make her available to perform there until the theatre agreed to pay an unprecedented $12,000 for six performances, plus travel expenses.*

dramatic sense that she could respect. That they worked well together was reflected on opening night in Maria's performance. As Bernstein described it, "The place was out of its mind. Callas? She was pure electricity."

Chicago Comes to Life

By 1954, not only had Maria transformed herself from operatic to balletic, she was ready for her second return to America. The Met was still refusing to pay her more than $1000 per performance, but Lawrence Kelly and Carol Fox in Chicago did not have such problems. Since Eddie Bagarozy's attempt to launch the United States Opera Company, Chicago had not been able to bring its opera scene to life. Kelly and Fox were two young concert organizers with this goal in mind and the means to succeed. They realized that not only was Maria the sort of international star that would put a definite shine on their city's opera house, but her story was one that Americans would respond to. She had been born in the USA; she had pulled herself to the top of her profession by hard work and gumption. The Chicagoans bent over backwards to get Maria. They agreed to her choice of repertoire (*Norma, Traviata* and *Lucia*), her cast (Tito Gobbi, Giuseppe di Stefano and Nicola Rossi-Lemeni, among others with whom she had worked over the years), and finally they agreed to Meneghini's asking price of $12,000 for six performances, as well

as travel expenses for diva and husband.

With Maria's appearance in Chicago, the Lyric Opera was launched in a glorious fashion. Even before she arrived in the States, the newspapers were awash in stories in stories of La Callas. There was much for editors and writers to work with: the "up by her own bootstraps" angle, the "ugly duckling" angle, the "Washington Heights girl returning home" angle, and many more. All of this meant that, even before she sang a single note of Norma, she was treated as a hero. After the opening night of her first American opera, her status was secure, as Claudia Cassidy's words in the *Chicago Tribune* reveal, "For my money she was not only up to specifications, she surpassed them...."

Cassidy would play an important role in the building of the Callas legend, and Maria came to have a great deal of respect for her knowledge and professionalism. The writer seemed to grasp the core of Maria's artistic intent. The title of the review she wrote for *Lucia,* Maria's final Chicago opera was, "Question: Which Is Mad, the Callas Lucia or Her Frenzied Public?" The copy went on, "Near pandemonium broke out. There was an avalanche of applause, a roar of cheers growing steadily louder and a standing ovation, and the aisles were full of men pushing as close to the stage as possible. I am sure they wished for bouquets to throw, a carriage to pull through the streets. Myself, I wish they had had both."

After the twenty-two curtain calls at the final performance of *Lucia,* the audience barely allowed Maria to escape. When asked her thoughts about

An ecstatic Maria poses for a press photograph with the chorus of Lucia *in Chicago, 1954. The audience's reaction caused* Chicago Tribune *critic Claudia Cassidy to wonder, "Which is mad, the Callas Lucia or her frenzied public?"*

America's reaction to her, she responded, "There is justice. I have had it. There is God. I have been touched by God's finger."

While Maria felt vindicated and victorious after her return to Chicago, there was something shadowing her from her not-too-distant past. She had forgotten the contract she had signed with Eddie Bagarozy in 1947 as she left New York for Italy. Even at the time, she had not given it serious consideration. He now claimed that he was owed $300,000 for expenses incurred upon Maria's behalf, as her sole representative. Nicola Rossi-Lemeni had signed a similar agreement with Bagarozy and managed to get out of it after paying a few thousand dollars. Meneghini, however, would not consider paying a dime. Maria issued a public denial of the claim and said that Bagarozy had obtained the contract under duress and had done nothing to help her career. It was in America, then, that Maria was shown both sides of success: the adulation of the crowds and the anger of those left behind.

Pursuing Visconti

While the contractual squabbles were playing themselves out in the background, Maria returned to Italy reborn. When she walked into La Scala

Maria receives congratulatory flowers from Meneghini in London, 1954.

for the first time, she ran into Toscanini, who on seeing the svelte, blonde vision before him said, "What have you done with all that weight? How did you make yourself so beautiful?" And just as she had managed to change herself dramatically, it was Maria's intention to do the same to opera. It had been a while since she worked with Visconti, but since *Il turco* she had not forgotten him. In the meantime her relationship with Serafin had declined as she went from the fat girl who needed a mentor to the beautiful woman who needed a visionary to push her art to the next level. Serafin remained the conductor with whom she made some of her finest recordings, but the "visionary" was to be Visconti. He was born in Milan and often said that he felt as if he had grown up at La Scala. He created a world on the stage that allowed Maria to loom larger even as she had grown physically smaller.

Although his aristocratic family had long had a box in the first tier at La Scala, it is unlikely that he would have been welcomed back as a director. Between his homosexuality and his

Maria rehearsing Vestale *with director Luchino Visconti, 1954.*

ing lack of propriety with which she pursued her crush on Visconti. She would rush into Biffi Scala, the restaurant nearest the opera house, search him out and if he was not present storm out ignoring everyone else. Maria was particularly jealous of Franco Corelli, a young tenor new to the Scala stage. As Visconti noted later, "Maria began to fall in love with me. Like so many Greeks she has a possessive streak and there were many terrible jealous scenes. She hated Corelli because he was handsome. It made her nervous—she was wary of beautiful people. She was always watching to see I didn't give him more attention than I gave her."

In fact, the thirty-year-old Maria behaved like an adolescent girl, and in doing so she often seemed to actually forget her husband. The older, grayer, boring and business-like Titta rarely inspired her as he previously had, though neither of them seemed to notice or mind. Meanwhile, *La vestale* was generating its own rumors and excitement. Everything from the Maria's dramatics off stage to the 80-million-lire budget fanned the public's expectations —expectations that, it should be noted, were met and then some. The grandiose, three-dimensional sets and exotic costumes were stunning, but it was Callas who sealed the deal. It was her performance, her ability to pick the proper tone and shade of voice, along with the precise gesture to complete the dramatic moment, and her deep, personal sense of the dramatic (even when out of character) that won the day. When showered with carnations at the curtain calls,

Communism, there were many reasons for the Milanese establishment to dislike him. Maria ignored all of that, however, and when she chose Spontini's *La vestale* to open La Scala's season, she did so with Visconti in mind. Indeed, it seems she often had Visconti in mind. Unlike her earlier relationships with mentors, Trevelli, de Hidalgo and Serafin, Maria developed a crush on Visconti despite his homosexuality. The fact that in her new body she felt a confidence and security in her femininity was probably related to the amaz-

Maria picked one of them up and, bowing to Toscanini who was in a stage box, presented it to him. This image of respect drove the house wild.

"They Want My Blood"

Although Maria was at the top of her game, 1955 was the year that indicated troubles ahead. Her first opera of the year was to be *Il trovatore*, but Mario del Monaco, who was to be Manrico and who was at the height of his popularity, succeeded in convincing Ghiringhelli to put on Giordano's *Andrea Chénier* instead. Del Monaco had had a great success with *Chénier* at the Met three weeks earlier. It had been a while since Maria had been truly tested, but she dove into the challenge of learning the part of Maddalena di Coigny in just five days. Of course, Maria was not quite in the physical shape she had once been. She was much thinner now, but the loss of so much weight so quickly must have had some effect on her health. Add to this that after so many successes there were plenty of people who were looking for any flaw, regardless of its size or significance. It was in her big aria, *"La mamma morta,"* that their patience was rewarded. Maria lost control of the climactic high B and the result was that her detractors in the audience drowned out her supporters with their hooting, booing and whistling. Whether or not the Tebaldi bloc had anything to do with this, Maria was convinced they had. So upsetting was

the fracas that even the backstage congratulations of the composer's widow could not dull the pain. Nor could the kind words of published critics like Emilio Radius, who wrote that Maria's performance "would have left the good Giordano openmouthed with admiration."

"They want my blood" was what Maria said about the Tebaldi faction. If Titta was unable to inspire love's glow in his wife as she pursued Visconti, he did manage to fan the flames of her paranoia. Tebaldi was the focus of her suspicions, and it was during this time that Maria was at her most openly ugly and nasty. Even if much of what was reported in pursuit of good copy was manipulated by the press, the public believed what they read. They reveled in Maria's comments, such as, "If the time comes when my dear friend Renata Tebaldi sings Norma or Lucia one night, then Violetta, La Gioconda or Medea the next—then and only then will we be rivals. Otherwise it is like comparing champagne with cognac. No—with Coca Cola."

Once again the Tebaldists and Callasites marshaled their forces. Not since Brazil a few years earlier had the enmity been this intense. If things had gotten out of hand in Mexico and South America, they were even worse in Italy. When Maria opened in *Medea* in Rome she found herself harassed by bass Boris Christoff, who throughout the preparation for the show had been infuriated by what he considered to be excessive rehearsals demanded by Maria. At the end of the opera he stepped in front of her, blocking her solo bow with his own considerable girth. She had no choice but to step back and fume.

Her next opera was to be *La sonnambula*, directed by Visconti and conducted by Bernstein. Unfortunately the previous several months had taken its toll on Maria and the doctor ordered her to take bed rest, so the opening was postponed for two weeks. Visconti and Bernstein were both perfectionists and as such worked extremely well together. They relished the extra time, but Maria grew jealous of Bernstein and his time with Visconti. Not only did she keep track of all of Visconti's movements from her hotel room, she made quite clear her intentions

Maria in Andrea Chénier, *La Scala, 1954. Although the role of Maddalena is secondary in the opera, Callas made the most of it, both dramatically and vocally. She sang it only six times.*

when Visconti and Bernstein visited her at the hotel. As they were leaving, Visconti later said, Maria commanded, "You stay here! I don't want you going off with Lenny again!"

But when it came time to perform, the jealous adolescent became the deferential student. Despite the fact that she had an innate sense of dramatic timing, Maria needed constant encouragement and confirmation of her enormous talents. This was the vital role Meneghini had played since 1947, but now Maria craved this attention from Visconti. She even engineered his presence on stage during performances—in a way. He later described it: "I always kept a handkerchief in my pocket with a drop of a particular English perfume on it, and Maria loved the scent. She told me always to place the handkerchief on the divan on which she had to lie down during the inn scene. 'That way I'll be able to walk directly to it with my eyes closed.' And so that's how we accomplished this effect. Luckily no musician in the orchestra ever decided to wear the same perfume, or one night she might have walked right off the stage and into the pit."

"I Will Not Be Sued"

The next two years were full of more victories for Maria. Among them was Tebaldi's decision not to appear on La Scala's stage (she would not return until 1959), where Callas ruled; her success in the comic *Il turco* at La Scala and the

Maria and Nicola Rossi-Lemeni in Il Turco in Italia, *La Scala, 1955. This was her first comic role, and it was a surprise success.*

beginning of a lifelong friendship with Franco Zeffirelli; brilliant performances in Berlin and other European cities; and, perhaps most importantly, a growing popularity in America. Her importance to the Lyric Opera of Chicago can't be underestimated: Lawrence Kelly would agree to practically anything to get her under contract. Indeed, the management of the Lyric Opera even agreed to assume full responsibility for protecting her against legal proceedings by Bagarozy, which were still ongoing. This was something that they would soon regret.

Maria committed herself not only to her performances, but to a round of cocktail parties, dinner parties, luncheons and other social events. The result was observed by Roger Dettmer, the music critic for the *Chicago American*: "The Town, we all know, has been Callas-crazy for more than a year, and none has been more demented than I. In the proper role and in good voice, I adore the woman; I am a slave in her spell."

But nothing is perfect, the last night of the final opera of the Chicago season, *Madama But-*

Maria, with Giuseppe di Stefano, in the title role in Puccini's Madama Butterfly, *Chicago 1955.*

terfly, was quite eventful. Actually, this third performance had been unscheduled and Lawrence Kelly and Carol Fox had pleaded with Maria to do one more before leaving. She agreed, and the resulting hysteric adulation of the audience seemed to confirm that she and they had made the right decision. When she was finally able to leave the stage, Maria was exhausted. Not long after she returned to her dressing room the real drama began. Marshal Stanley Pringle and Deputy Sheriff Dan Smith had managed to get around the cordon that the Lyric's management had put around Callas. In their fedoras and raincoats they looked as if they'd stepped out of the latest noir thriller, and when they burst into her room Maria was caught utterly off guard. Still in Cio-Cio-San's kimono, she was initially shocked and silent. They were there to serve her with Eddie Bagarozy's summons, and did so with enthusiasm.

Furious, Maria exclaimed with the tone of the goddesses she had been portraying so effectively for years, "I will not be sued! I have the voice of an angel! No man can sue me!" It is safe to assume that the marshal had faced down more real-life dangers than the one Maria affected, and he calmly stuck the summons into her kimono and turned to leave. Unfortunately for Maria there were photographers around and one of them caught her in her fury, accentuated by the garish stage make-up she was still wearing. The treachery she felt was deep. "I couldn't have been betrayed worse," she wrote to the wife of EMI's Dario Soria.

Upon her return to Milan, the horror that had begun in Chicago continued. She was faced with advertisements in local newspapers claiming that she had lost her weight by eating Pantanella's "psychological macaroni." So began another battle: while she was fighting Bagarozy in America, she was fighting what came to be known as "the battle of the spaghetti" in Italy.

If her clash with Tebaldi had barely cast a glancing blow on her image (in fact, it probably helped her, as the public eagerly picked sides and bought LPs by the millions), her years of

Arriving at Idlewild Airport on October 15, 1956, for her long awaited debut at the Metropolitan Opera.

media-inundated world that we know was just being born, and Maria was, in many ways, the first electronic media star. Accordingly, she was able to arouse stronger feelings than any living singer had before, as the jealousy, covetousness and resentment matched her "me against the world" state of mind that Meneghini had facilitated for so long.

Despite the ugliness there were still victories to come for La Callas. Just before she appeared in *Trovatore* in Chicago the year before, an agreement was finally reached with the Met. Just as Ghirighelli's hand had been forced by Maria's major successes in Florence, Rudolf Bing could hardly stick to his "never pay an artist more than $1000 for a performance" rule, particularly after her two successful seasons in Chicago, her history-making performances at La Scala, appearances in Covent Garden, Berlin, Vienna, Mexico City...the list continued to grow. When Maria landed at Idlewild Airport (now JFK) on October 15, 1956, her father, godfather and a good deal of New York City was there to greet her. *Time* magazine ran a cover story about her, and in preparation for the article, had distributed a questionnaire to both friends and enemies. The results added to the growing anti-Callas feeling. The most effective bit of ugliness in the article was the quote they got from Evangelia. In it she excerpted a section of the last letter she had received from Maria: "Don't come to me with your troubles. I had to work for my money and you are young enough to work too. If you can't make enough

success were beginning to work against her. After the publication of the photo of the enraged, vicious-looking Maria in Chicago, the press was more than willing to use her to drive paper sales. Rumors about her were now accepted without any of the consideration that they might have been given before. As things heated up for her outside the opera hall, they started to intensify inside as well. In the late 1950s, the money to live on, you can jump out the window or drown yourself."

The image of the tigress could not have been better served. Not only was Maria's relationship with her mother dredged up, Time dug into her dealings with her peers. Tenor Giuseppe di Stefano, whose relationship with Maria had hit a low point, was quoted as saying, "I'm never going to sing opera with her again and that's final." The fact that opera singers were by their very natures dramatic and hyperbolic did not make a difference. In fact, it was very much a self-fulfilling prophecy: the more hullabaloo, the more audience, the more audience, the more hullabaloo.

Opening night of *Norma* proved this. Many in the audience came not so much to hear Maria as to react to Maria. The cold, heartless woman they had read so much about met a very unsympathetic audience. Callas was not unaffected by this. That night she was, unsurprisingly, petrified. The stage manager, Dino Yannopoulos, had to shove her onstage, saying, "I promised to deliver a prima donna and so I will; after that it's up to you."

He must have known how motivated Maria would be by those words. Her entire career had been up to her. Despite the terror she felt at facing the audience from the one internationally significant stage she had not yet conquered, Maria rose to the challenge. Through *Norma,* Maria was able to unleash the spectacular artistry that newspaper and magazine reports could never drown out. By the second act, she had begun to capture them. By the end of the opera,

the formerly cold, unsympathetic audience demanded sixteen curtain calls. The Callas magic seemed to work once again, but the critics were not as convinced as the audience was. Her vocal limitations were the focus of most reviewers—the veiled middle register, the deficiencies of tone—and this certainly stole some of the glow.

Regardless of the less than stellar reviews, following the opening night there were several magnificent social events through which she was introduced to the Jet-Set world. A particularly important player in this realm was gossip columnist Elsa Maxwell, who also happened to be a leader of the pro-Tebaldi faction. A close friend of Renata's, Maxwell set forth with the intention of making Maria's stay a difficult one. She referred to Callas as "the devious diva" and in her articles attacked her from every angle. For example, Maxwell wrote of Maria's opening *Lucia*: "I confess the great Callas acting in the Mad Scene left me completely unmoved.... I was intrigued by the red wig she wore through the first two acts but in the Mad Scene she came on as a platinum blonde. Why this change of color? What did it mean to this egocentric extrovert?"

This was also the point at which the reticent Tebaldi herself joined the. In a letter to *Time,* she replied to the charge, reportedly from Maria herself, "She's got no backbone. She's not like Callas." In her response Renata wrote, "The signora says that I have no backbone. I reply that I have one great thing that she has not—a heart." This charge hit a major sore spot in the two factions. Those who followed Tebaldi loved her warmth and outgoing personality and her beautiful, unchallengin, voice, and those who were pro-Callas loved not only the risks she took with her singing and the spectacular manner in which she took those risks, but her fiery temperament and refusal to accept anything but the best.

Romancing Maxwell

Maria's successes had brought her to the point where only further successes would allow her to continue. Besides, as she became more comfortable in her new body, she needed more outlets for her femininity. She realized that opinion-maker Elsa Maxwell was the linchpin for all of this. To have Maxwell on her side would not only ease the professional battles she faced, but would open for her doors in society that were not easily opened. But winning Maxwell over would not be easy, as Maxwell herself let it be known: "I look like a bulldog and I have a dog's persistence."

Maxwell not only wrote about the international rich but she entertained them. The seventy-three-year-old writer had been known

Maria and Meneghini with American gossip columnist Elsa Maxwell, visiting Venice Lido. Maxwell developed a crush on Maria, and Maria used that to her advantage in establishing a fan base in the United States.

for her flamboyant parties for decades. In her autobiography she wrote, "I have been called a parasite for accepting the largesse of the wealthy, but I contributed as much, at least, as I received. I had imagination and they had money, a fair exchange of the commodity possessed by each side in the greatest abundance." Through all of her years of fabulousness, whether in Paris, New York, Venice or Monte Carlo, it was well known that Maxwell had little romantic interest in men. Maria seemed to take advantage of this fact and when Greek film tycoon Spyros Skouras invited her and Titta to a dinner dance given for the American Hellenic Welfare Fund at the Waldorf-Astoria just a few days before they were to return to Milan, she knew that she must take advantage of the opportunity presented.

Maria knew that Elsa Maxwell would be in attendance and when the moment came she asked Skouras to introduce her. At that moment the Callas charm, which could bring down entire opera houses, was focused on Maxwell. "I esteem you," she told her, "as a lady of honesty who is devoted to telling the truth." This exchange was, of course, reported in Maxwell's next column. She continued, "When I looked into her amazing eyes, which are brilliant, beautiful and hypnotic, I realized she is an extraordinary person." It was, it seems, love at first sight. It is telling how simple it was for Maria to supplant Tebaldi as Maxwell's favorite, and also telling that she was careful not to be left alone with her new fairy godmother for even a few minutes. Regardless of how obvious her manipulations were, Maxwell

fell for them, and made certain that Maria's name was rarely out of the public's consciousness.

International café society beckoned and Maria dove in. She returned to New York after the Christmas holiday and prepared for a party at the Waldorf-Astoria with the theme of a "regal pageant." Wisely playing up both her exotic beauty and her personality, Maria went as Hatshepshut, the Egyptian queen, wearing $3 million worth of emeralds. She put as much energy into this costume as she would the clothing for any opera, and Elsa Maxwell, who appeared as Catherine the Great (make of that what you will), certainly responded. After New York, Callas gave a concert in Chicago, forgetting that she had foresworn the city a short time earlier, and then went back to Milan for an appearance at La Scala. She made a splash at both of these events sporting glamorous ensembles. She had begun to travel with Toy, the perfect toy poodle, and accessories like chinchilla coats and diamond-encrusted glasses accentuated the prima donna glamour. Her star had risen so high that she no longer had to sing to bring the house down.

From Milan she went to London to perform Norma, where the *Daily Mail* devoted three columns just to the preparations for her arrival at Covent Garden and the Savoy. At Covent Garden Maria had the successes that she could not find at the Met. After her second act duet, *"Mira o Norma,"* with mezzo Ebe Stignani, conductor John Pritchard had no option but to break the house's rule against encores. The audience's torrential reaction demanded it. Following

Maria (right) in Anna Bolena *at* La Scala, *1958. When the role was resurrected in 1957 as a tribute to Donizetti, conductor Gianandrea Gavazzeni immediately recognized the tragic heroine as "an ideal vehicle for Maria Callas, both musically and theatrically."*

the performance, Rudolf Bing wired her his congratulations and she replied, "I am still trying to discover what happened in New York. I am only sorry I couldn't give you personally what other theaters have. I hope next year."

Maria was on something of a roll, and this was despite her continuing vocal problems. Ultimately, however, just as an old boxer is more dangerous than a young one because of his experience and knowledge of the ring, Callas continued to stun audiences with the virtuosity of her per-

formances despite their flaws. In the premiere of *Anna Bolena* at La Scala in 1957, her fusion of singing and acting won her the longest solo curtain call the house had ever seen, twenty-four minutes. These professional victories, added to the social victories she had had in the year past, made her even more intriguing to glittering beau monde. The photo that appeared in Milanese newspapers of Elsa Maxwell in Maria's arms, taken at the Milan airport a few days after this premiere, says it all.

Commendatore

Meanwhile, Maria was preparing for what would be her final collaboration with Visconti, Gluck's *Iphigénie en Tauride*, her twentieth production at La Scala. Maria disagreed with Visconti's placement of the story in an elaborate eighteenth-century rococo context. "Why are you doing it like this? It's a Greek story and I'm a Greek woman, so I want to look Greek onstage."

Maria in Gluck's Iphigénie en Tauride, *La Scala, 1957.*

And so her argument went throughout rehearsals. Despite her dislike of his staging, her professionalism would not allow her to do less than her best. She entered during a storm scene, walking up a high staircase and then running down it trailed by a cloak twenty-five yards long. Visconti remembered, "Every night she hit her high note on the eighth step, so extraordinarily coordinated was her music and movement. She was like a circus horse, conditioned to pull off any theatrical stunt she was taught." This commitment to her art was awarded by Italian President Gronchi when he conferred upon her the honorary title of Commendatore.

It only seems right that she have some sort of official title just as she was beginning to socialize with aristocrats. Shortly after Maria became a Commendatore, Elsa Maxwell toasted her in Paris with tea with the Windsors, cocktails with the Rothschilds, dinner at Maxim's and a day at the races with the legendary playboy Ali Khan, son of Aga Khan and former husband of Rita Hayworth. While all of this socializing was certainly fabulous it was also nearly as exhausting as performing. She was drained the time came for her to make her first appearance in Athens after twelve years.

If New York City was a tough nut to crack, Athens promised to be even tougher. Evangelia's accusations against her daughter carried even greater weight there, and some felt that the Greek government was wasting its money on opera when there were poor people to feed. In order to avoid controversy, the government arranged to fly Evangelia and Jackie to America during Maria's visit. Nevertheless, it was not a comfortable homecoming for Maria. She did not feel strong enough, or in good enough form, to face down and seduce an audience as she had at the Met. She was stuck, because she knew that canceling would only inspire greater anger, but after an extended period of stalling she finally cancelled her first performance. This vacillation is apparently native to Greece; the government followed suit and did not actually announce the cancellation until an hour before curtain time.

When she appeared five nights later she did not have to contend with mere irritation and disapproval, but rage. Once again the Callas charm worked its magic and the audience's iciness melted under it. When she finished her last aria, the Mad Scene from Ambroise Thomas's

Hamlet, the crowd broke out into booming applause and demanded an encore.

After Athens, Maria had La Scala's visit to the Edinburgh Festival before her. Her doctors, concerned with her low blood pressure and ever lessening weight (he collarbones stuck out whenever she wore an open dress), attempted to get her to cancel her appearances, but she knew how important it was for her to appear with the company. And foregoing her social obligations seemed similarly impossible. After all, what was the point of all of this work not to take advantage of the fascinating world to which it gave her access? Elsa Maxwell's ball in Venice, in Maria's honor, was just that sort of event.

But first, off she went to cold and cloudy Scotland. Maria opened the season there with *Sonnambula* and despite her exhaustion, managed

Maria as La sonnambula, *La Scala 1958. Maria's by now girlish figure was perfect for the tender character of Amina, a role for which her voice teacher Elvira de Hidalgo was once known. During the production, designer Piero Tosi recalls, she wore a very tight corset: "I tell you it would kill a film star!"*

to make it through the four performances required of her. The problem came when Ghiringhelli announced a fifth performance, despite the fact that Maria had told him she would only do four. He seems to have thought that by announcing an additional show, he could force her to perform. That is not what happened. Maria left and the British press, unaware of the circumstances, or perhaps just not very interested in them, tagged it "Another Callas walk-out." Most of the people on the inside, including the Lord Provost of Edinburgh, understood, but the press was not sympathetic. Of course, that she was leaving dreary Edinburgh and opera for sunny Venice and a fabulous party did not help. If Maria was so exhausted, how could she manage to find the energy for a party? The photos from Venice showed a Maria brimming with happiness and life. Elsa Maxwell did not help matters when she wrote in her column, "I have had many presents in my life… but I have never had any star give up a performance in an opera house because she felt she was breaking her word to a friend."

Enter Onassis

The problem was that after 22 *Sonnambulas*, 52 *Traviatas*, 41 *Lucias* and 73 *Normas*, along with the other 28 roles she had performed since 1947, opera did not hold the same excitement for Maria that the Jet-Set world did. While opera fans might not have seen the glamorous nightlife

as a worthwhile use of a diva's time, the diva began to see it quite differently.

The Venice party would prove life-changing for Maria. Present at the gala event was another Greek of significance, Aristotle Socrates Onassis. He attended with his wife, Tina. Despite the fact that she was quite beautiful, Onassis's eyes followed Maria more than they should have, even given her status. It was not long before he had maneuvered himself to Maria's side and begun making small talk. He offered her a boat and two seamen to ferry her about while she was in Venice, and for the rest of her time there he managed to appear wherever she was. After her long-unrequited crush on Visconti, this was the first time a man showered such attention upon her. Meneghini was present, of course, just as Tina Onassis was, but it did not stop either Maria or Aristotle from flirting.

After her fabulous Venetian holiday and her exciting new conquest, Maria's return to Milan was something else. Ghiringhelli refused to issue a public statement that would clear her name and the Edinburgh disappearance was added to her growing list of crimes. It was not merely the public that was angry with Maria; friends like Wally Toscanini took her to task as well. She was next scheduled to be the opening of the San Francisco opera season. Once again her doctors argued that she must allow her body to recover from the hectic rounds of performance and partying, and this time she was ready to listen.

The wisdom of canceling a performance when she was still being blasted for Edinburgh was certainly something to consider, but "considering" was not something Maria was prone to do. She agreed, and a few days before the much-publicized opening night, she sent a telegram to the director of the San Francisco Opera canceling the September appearances, but offering to honor the agreed-upon October ones. Adler was enraged and not only cancelled all of her scheduled performances, but referred the case to the American Guild of Musical Artists. He did so because Maria had set herself up once again to seem like a willful party girl rather than a serious professional artist. There are few problems more difficult to fix than that of perception, and the public's perception was being fueled by a growing litany of Callas's cancellations and court appearances.

Case Closed

Not long after this, Maria and Meneghini quietly finally finished the Bagarozy case by settling out of court just as Nicola Rossi-Lemeni had done years earlier. Because the terms were never made public it is unknown whether Meneghini's greed and Maria's paranoia brought things to a better close than if the whole drama had never been played out. Regardless, the case, and their hard-headed approach to it, had engendered more bad feelings about Maria.

As if cursed, or perhaps stemming from her waning interest in working so hard, Callas continued to make missteps, find her body

uncooperative, or both. From this point in her career, though she was still capable of giving brilliant performances on stage, soon after something would occur that would supply her detractors with more ammunition. Maria returned to Italy and prepared to go back to La Scala. From the beginning, it was clear that Edinburgh was still in the public's consciousness and that Ghiringhelli would not make a statement and clear her name. Professional bickering would only add to this toxic mix, and di Stefano, despite his declaration to the world through the Time article that he would never perform with her again, was to be Riccardo to her Amelia in *Un ballo in maschera*.

Maria in Un ballo in maschera, *1956-1957 season, La Scala.*

At Tour d'Argent, Paris, 1958. In this time period Maria basked fully in the attention paid her by cafe society. On several occasions, she was accused by the public and the media of putting more energy into her nightlife than her performances.

The Show Must Go On

That she was the unchallenged Queen of La Scala only raised the pressure on her and the ire of her enemies. Maria rose to the challenge every time and she continued to redefine new role, and electrify audiences in ones she had performed before. After Milan, she went to Rome for *Norma*. As always, there was a good deal of nightlife, and she was seen celebrating the New Year at an exclusive Roman nightclub. The rumor mills spun with tales of her late night, and everyone debated whether she came home at 1:20 A.M., 2:00 A.M., or later. This sort of focus must have been difficult to bear, but Maria had essentially placed herself where she was. One does not become the Queen of La Scala accidentally. Of course, when the Queen has been out partying and wakes up three days before a gala opening without her voice, with a sold-out house that includes the President of Italy, it is easy to see how her subjects might become unsympathetic. This is precisely what happened and this amazingly strong willed woman was faced with a united front: the show must go on.

By the evening of the premiere, Maria had regained some of her voice, but from the moment she began she knew she was in trouble. The audience was silent at first, seemingly shocked by what was unfolding before them. As her voice slipped and her dramatically lackluster performance continued, the crowd began to speak. "Go back to Milan!" shouted someone. "You've cost us a million lire!" said someone else. At intermission, Maria decided that she could not finish. Despite the fact that the opera house had known for three days about her condition they had never seriously considered that Maria would not be able to perform. Indeed, they had not bothered to arrange for an understudy.

All Maria knew was that she could not finish the performance. She was exhausted and in pain. Her inner circle, Margherita Wallmann, Elsa Maxwell, tried to convince her to stay at the opera house, but she left and, understanding the audience's reaction to such a move, she wisely chose to take an underpass that led directly to her hotel. Meanwhile, a very angry public was gathering in the streets. Knowing that she was staying at the Hotel Quirinale, they surrounded it, hurling angry abuse up at her windows. The pro- and anti-Callas factions were actually coming to blows. The next morning's newspapers reflected the crowd's mood. *Il Giorno* said, "Italian by her marriage, Milanese because of the unfounded admiration of certain segments of La Scala's audience, international because of her dangerous relationship with Elsa Maxwell, [she] has for several years followed a path of melodramatic debauchery. This episode shows that Maria Meneghini Callas is also a disagreeable performer who lacks the most elementary sense of discipline and propriety."

It was five days before Maria felt physically well and emotionally strong enough to leave her room. Everyone from Visconti to the wife

Maria arrives in New York to perform La traviata *at the Met, after stunning the press and public by canceling a performance of* Norma *after the first act in Rome and causing a near riot by angry fans.*

of the President contacted her the following day to tell her that they understood the situation. Of course, that did not stop politicians from denouncing her in parliament or the opera house from asking the prefecture of Rome for an order banning Maria from completing the three remaining performances of *Norma*.

The debacle in Rome fueled Maria's growing paranoia. It also underlined something that was at the root of many of her other problems: singing was not fun any more, but she could

not stop. Although she had an entirely new social world around her, she knew that her place in it was based on her talents as a singer. Meanwhile, people like Ghiringhelli, who had never liked her and were not subtle in their opposition to her, were able to use the circumstances to their benefit.

Luckily for her, Maria's next performances were in America, where it would be easier to put that night in Rome behind her, and a six-hour stopover in Paris helped set the tone for the coming months. At Maxim's, the chef created a dish just for her, and they set a transistor radio beside her plate so that she could listen to her *Trovatore,* which was being broadcast on French radio. No detail was too small and, as *Le Figaro* put it, "Paris gave Maria the welcome it reserves for sovereigns and honored profits." The Queen was once more in state.

Besides her performance in Chicago, she also had the American Guild of Musical Artists hearing to contend with. Before the twenty-

Despite the bad press she was receiving in Europe, the Met audience welcomed her La traviata *with a standing ovation, 1957.*

man tribunal, Maria spent two hours defending her professional reputation. The result was not a suspension but a reprimand. In other words, her professionalism was noted, but her peers had warned her that they were watching her behavior.

From Chicago, doubtless relieved, Maria went to New York and performed to raves, in spite of the uninspired sets and costumes and an unimpressive cast. Knowing that she was under close observation she avoided displays of temper and worked with the focus that only she had. The result may not have been the perfect *Traviata,* but it was the truest Violetta that New York had ever seen, and the resulting 30 minutes of curtain calls proved it.

Ups and Downs

Through the rest of 1957 and into 1958, Maria steadily reasserted herself as opera's reigning diva. From Paris to Rome—where she faced down her detractors and had people screaming her name in the streets, in contrast to the prior year's baleful animosity. Her tour of American cities showed the world what Callas could do. Regrettably, this period included some bumps as well. After re-conquering Rome, she found Ghiringhelli to be even less friendly. She sought to bring him around as she had done with the Roman mobs: and not by sweet-talking him. At La Scala, playing Imogene in the final scene of *Il pirata,* she turned and spat, *"La...vedete...il palco funesto"* ("There, behold, the fateful scaffold") at Ghiringhelli's empty box. In Italian, *"palco"* means both scaffold and box, and her meaning was not lost on anyone. The General Manager of La Scala had the final word, though, and as the audience showered her with cheers and flowers he ordered the safety curtain dropped, abruptly ending the accolades. She announced that it was the end of her relationship with La Scala. All Ghiringelli said when asked about the loss of Callas was, "The prima donnas pass, La Scala remains."

As upsetting as this was for Maria, she still had a huge audience. Her American tour and her concerts in England, France and Holland in 1958 proved it. She left New York after some brilliant performances, but she and Rudolf Bing had not come to terms on what she would appear in next at the Met. It was partially a matter of greed—Bing would not pay what Callas wanted—and partially artistic sensibility. Nothing that the Met offered inspired her and, after the dreary *Traviata* she had been forced to contend with (which arguably allowed her to glow more brightly because of the dull backdrop it provided), she was suspicious of what she would find when she got there. Meneghini, who was famous for his derisive negotiations, certainly did not help. Ultimately, Bing wired Maria in Dallas as she was preparing for the premiere of *Medea* and demanded that she confirm the latest schedule he had offered by 10:00 the next morning. "La Divina" would not be pressured, and probably not believing that anyone would refuse her, ignored the due date. The next night, only hours before the curtain was to rise, another telegram from Bing arrived, this one formally informing her that her contract with the Metropolitan Opera was being cancelled.

Rudolf Bing, director of the Metropolitan Opera, congratulates Maria after a Chicago performance of Il trovatore. *Soon thereafter, miscommunications would lead to a canceled contract and an angry rift between Bing and "La Divina."*

It seemed as if the greatest opera houses in the world were too small for the Queen; yet perhaps that was entirely the point. Maria no longer needed the major houses because she had the entire world as a stage. As she grew weary of her professional life and more entranced by her social life, maybe lesser-known houses would allow her greater liberty. At the same time, it would permit these houses access to a star that they might not have otherwise been able to attract. In this way, Maria brought great opera to a much larger world. And, in an era captivated by popular culture personalities like Marilyn Monroe and Elvis Presley, Maria Callas was not only changing the way operas were performed but expanding their audience.

"But She Is Already Married"

The end of 1958 saw her debut in Paris, a city which had long had a great affection for Maria. She would perform at a charity gala for the Legion d'Honneur with the likes of Charlie Chaplin, Jean Cocteau, the Windsors, Brigitte Bardot and Emile de Rothschild. Tickets were the costliest ever at L'Opéra. Also in the audience would be Aristotle Onassis, who sent a huge bunch of red roses with a note in Greek the morning of the performance. Another bunch, again with best wishes in Greek, arrived at lunch, and just as she was leaving for the opera house, another. She remarked to Titta how romantic Onassis was, but said little else about it.

Later in 1959, they ran into Onassis and his wife Tina in Venice at another ball and this time he invited them aboard his yacht, the *Christina*. Maria made polite excuses, saying that she would be leaving for Covent Garden and Onassis quickly replied that they were planning on attending. This surprised Mrs. Onassis not because she knew of no plan to be in London—a man of Onassis's wealth went where and when he pleased—but because she knew that he had no interest in opera. In fact he detested it.

Aristotle Onassis was not a man to do things in a small, quiet way. A millionaire shipping tycoon with fingers in hundreds of financial pies, he led the life that defined the 1960s Jet Set. Accordingly, he did not just buy tickets and go to the opera with his wife in London, but organized a party of 37 people. It was the first time he saw Maria through an entire opera and it clearly held his interest. Afterwards he took his guests, who included Randolph Churchill, Margot Fonteyn and Cecil Beaton, to a grand party in Maria's honor at the Dorchester ballroom, which he had had decorated entirely in pink and filled with pink roses. The generosity of her host and abundance of all things impressed Maria deeply. While Onassis was unattractive, indeed, frog-like, he had a vitality, energy and elegance that made him seem more handsome than the other men in the room. She left the party at 3:00 in the morning having had a wonderful time, and posed for a photograph with Titta and Onassis in a triple embrace.

Meanwhile, the invitations to take a cruise

on the *Christina* kept coming from both Aristotle and Tina. Meneghini was understandably hesitant, even claiming that he could not go to sea because he needed to stay in touch with his ill mother. Onassis, however, assured him there would be no trouble, because "there are forty-two radio telephones on the *Christina*."

A few weeks later the Meneghini-Callases found themselves on a plane bound for Monte Carlo where the *Christina* was docked. They were joined there by Mr. and Mrs. Onassis; Sir Winston and Lady Churchill, their daughter Diana and his secretary Anthony Montague Browne; Lord Moran, Churchill's doctor; and Umberto Agnelli, the head of Fiat, and his wife. If the ship itself was amazing in its grandeur—solid-gold fixtures in every bathroom, each of which were completely marbled; a lapis lazuli fireplace in the game room; an El Greco in the study; the oldest Buddha, covered with jewels, known to exist in the West; a swimming pool decorated with a reproduction of a mosaic from the Palace of Knossos—the company was equally impressive. The last time Maria had seen Churchill had been when she was a teenager and he had come to Athens for negotiations during the Greek Civil War. In this stunning setting, surrounded by wealth, luxury and legendary company, Onassis turned his charms on Maria.

Meneghini and Callas dine with Aristotle Onassis aboard his yacht, the Christina, *1958.*

Christina Onassis, Meneghini, and Maria aboard the Christina. *It was Meneghini who convinced Maria that the two should accept Onassis's fateful invitation, despite her indisposition.*

Although she could turn herself into a giggling, wondering girl when necessary, Maria was in her middle thirties and clearly knew what Onassis had in mind before she set foot on the *Christina.* She had arranged for her payment from a concert she had recently sung at the Holland Festival not to be deposited in the bank account she shared with Titta, but asked her friend Peter Diamond, the festival's director, to hold the money for her. Since losing weight and entering the world of the beautiful people, she had gained even greater confidence in her own womanly attributes. The little girl who never dared to hope that she might attract the attention of a knight in shining armor, which was

now waiting for her rescuer. Meneghini was nine years older than Onassis with none of his flair or vitality. At this point, his only interest seemed to be in managing Maria and tweaking anyone who wanted to book her for an appearance. He was more a factotum than a lover, and for the first time in her life she actually had some sense of what a lover might actually be.

In fact, Onassis's sense of the dramatic fit exquisitely into her own, which only made him more attractive. Not only could the two speak to each other in Greek, but he loved to tell stories from Greek mythology. When the ship anchored at the Turkish capital of Istanbul, which is still called Constantinople by the Greeks, they were received by the Patriarch of the Church. Maria and Aristotle received his blessings and were called by him, "the world's greatest singer and the greatest seaman of the modern world, the new Ulysses." Maria was ensnared. Poor Meneghini might have been a bore but he was not stupid. He was heard to mutter, "But she is already married."

Every time they stopped in a city during the cruise there was a party, and Istanbul was no different. Meneghini stayed on board, and when Maria returned she told him that she was in love with Onassis. The remainder of the trip was as awkward and strange as only such situations can be, but at its end, when Meneghini and Callas left on one of Onassis's private planes, it would be the last time the two ever flew as a couple again.

In the months that followed, the press pursued the story and found Maria demure, Aristotle proud, Tina silent and Titta, understandably, angry. Of course, Evangelia chimed in: "I was Maria's first victim. Now it's Meneghini. Onassis will be the third." She suggested that Maria would marry Onassis to further her limitless ambition. Even Elsa Maxwell, who had introduced the couple, sided with Tina and sounded more like an unrequited lover than a concerned friend. Soon, Tina took her two children and flew to her father's home in Paris. Aristotle pursued her, but only halfheartedly.

For Maria's part, she was sad to be ending her relationship with Titta, but she later said, "I had become prematurely dull and old.... Life for me really began at forty, or at least nearly

Kissing Meneghini in 1958, just months prior to their separation.

forty." Her life may have livened up with Ari, but she was an old-fashioned girl, and she wanted much more from him. The long hours she had spent making dinner for Meneghini had not been play-acting—she really wanted to have a family. Now that she'd met a man who appealed to her, the desire to have children, that she had expressed to her mother years earlier in Mexico City, came right back to her.

Evangelia had gotten it, as usual, quite wrong. It was not Maria's ambition for power and prestige that had driven her to Onassis, but her desire for a family with a man she felt passionately about and who she believed could return that emotion. As she would write to her godfather, "I want to live, just like a normal woman, with children, a home, a dog."

Disappointment and Distraction

Unfortunately, Onassis was a bad gamble for Maria. Men who have pulled themselves to the top tend to be far too self-involved to make good partners. Aristotle, who always told stories of his younger days of struggle with far more intensity than he spoke about his mature successes, got bored quickly. Once he was sure of Maria's love she was simply a beautiful, famous woman who sang. He teased her about it and, as they began to spend more and more time together, he would ask her why she still wanted to sing. Onassis had no interest in Callas's art and the pair of children he had had with Tina precluded any "need" to begin another family. The cards were stacked high against Maria for any permanent relationship, but she didn't realize it until it was too late.

Although Maria's desire to perform had been steadily decreasing over the previous two years and she had every excuse to stop, it defined her, and she couldn't bear to give it up completely. In 1959, the first year of the love affair, Maria sang several concerts, which took less preparation than an entire opera, and appeared on the

Maria and Onassis were hounded by photographers when they went public with their relationship, 1960.

opera stage only nine times. She even referred to a concert in Bilbao as "a silly little engagement." In 1960, at the height of the "romance," she did not even perform until July; after that she recorded a recital and a complete *Norma* and performed seven times. She spent more and more time aboard the *Christina* and it's pretty clear that she did not study scores when she and Ari retired for the evening. Franco Zeffirelli later referred to "a definite sexual passion" between the couple that seems to have displaced her passion for music. Aboard ship she spent time in the kitchen making expert comments on the chef's Greek dishes and began making herself known to the crew. Indeed, Maria spent

Maria and Onassis at the International Sporting Club in Monte Carlo, 1960.

more of the next five years acting as Onassis's "First Lady" than she did as "La Callas." For his part, Ari did his best to distract her from music. He arranged for his friend Carl Foreman to offer Maria a film role opposite Gregory Peck in *The Guns of Navarone,* which she turned down, and he tried to put together several other non-musical projects for her. As it turned out, she avoided all film projects until 1969 when she took the lead role in Pier Paolo Pasolini's *Medea,* based not on the opera but on the Greek legend. She wanted to find the right part and not appear foolish, a diva who had made a clumsy crossover into film.

It is easy to assume that Onassis's motivation in attempting to change her artistic focus was that it would make her more "accessible." Opera, i.e., high culture, can be intimidating to many people, whereas film is much more mainstream. This really was at the core of Onassis's problems with Maria. Her fame and glory, which were based on her great artistic gifts, put her on much higher cultural ground than he. He was a multimillionaire who owned fleets, an airline and myriad companies, who had a great deal of influence in Greece, Monte Carlo and several South American countries. All he had was money. He would probably have grown bored with Callas eventually anyway, but her unique gifts, and the fact that he could not compete with them, must have stirred a certain insecurity that he was not used to feeling, particularly when inspired by a woman.

Through all of this Maria just wanted to get

Maria and Grace Kelly attend a black-tie supper at the International Sporting Club to mark the closing of the second annual Monte Carlo Television Festival on the 19th of January, 1962. Just two years earlier, the Princess and Prince of Monaco had shunned Maria and Onassis in the wake of their public and highly publicized affair.

married and have his children. Between 1960 and 1965, she performed a mere fraction of the times she had in the prior five years, but she never forgot who she was and how she got there. While she would take whatever role Onassis gave her in his business life, she would never simply allow him to throw her into projects that she thought might blemish her artistic reputation. It was just this independence that may have marred her chances to get Ari to marry her.

Maria and Onassis dining at a Parisian restaurant, 1960. Their involvement marked the decline of her illustrious career. She was growing tired of her arduous schedule, and Onassis encouraged her to back away from performing, partially out of his lack of interest in opera, partially out of envy of her celebrity.

Triumphant Tosca

After eighteen months of absence, Maria returned to opera in an extraordinary way in 1964. Directors and opera houses had been coming to her with offers all along, but she had ignored them all. The questions about her voice (did she still have it?) built up to a furious crescendo. Rather than watch her artistic reputation fade away, she wrote to David Webster at Covent Garden telling him that she would finally do *Tosca,* but only if

it were to happen "now." This was her Zeffirelli period and she knew that he was there directing *Rigoletto,* and asked him to help her with *Tosca.* Zeffirelli was (and remained until her death) not only a great supporter of Maria's, but a dear friend with whom she shared a sympathetic artistic sensibility. It was certainly frightening to return to the opera house after so long, but with him directing her she was confident that she would be able to silence her critics and return to the top. A few years earlier she

Maria as Puccini's Tosca *at Covent Garden, London, 1964. After several years' absence from the stage, Maria began to miss performing and she made a welcome return.*

had begun re-training her ever-more-wayward voice—particularly the upper register—and some of her self-assurance had returned.

At first there was resistance at Covent Garden to initiating a new project while *Rigoletto* was ongoing, but Zeffirelli and Webster were so certain that it would be brilliant that soon everyone fell into line. Tito Gobbi was to play opposite Maria as Scarpia, and with Zeffirelli and his team created an amazing show, that would change the way *Tosca* would be performed thereafter. Doubtless, her growing disillusionment with Ari fueled her characterization of Tosca's suffering and jealousy. The audience and critical reactions were just as dramatic.

Maria returns to New York for a performance of Tosca *and is greeted with wild enthusiasm.*

Maria, with baritone Tito Gobbi, in Tosca *at Covent Garden, 1965.*

But what she wanted more than ever was simple: to be the mother of Aristotle Onassis's child. Her ongoing struggle to meet the demands of her art was at least something she could attempt to control. Her "simpler" need was utterly in Onassis's hands. Accordingly, she took refuge in her greater destiny. After the Covent Garden *Toscas,* she went on to Paris for a Zeffirelli *Norma,* which was an overall success despite some vocal problems (and the need to cancel the final act of the last performance), and in 1965 she made her long awaited return to the Met.

With Tito Gobbi again as Scarpia, Maria set forth to reconquer New York City, and with some relief and more than a little trepidation she found it quite ready to be conquered by her. The Met was sold out for weeks in advance, the tickets were kept in a safe and a banner proclaiming, WELCOME HOME, CALLAS, was hung on the front of the opera house. The distinguished center of high culture looked more

like the site of a Beatles concert, as with people queued up with sleeping bags, blankets and pillows more than two days before opening night. It had been seven years since she had last appeared at the Met, also as Tosca, but this time the stakes were even higher. On opening night the house was filled with celebrities including Bette Davis, Leonard Bernstein, and Edward, Robert and, ironically, Jacqueline Kennedy. Up until that point, their paths had not yet crossed.

Although the audience was taken with the heroic widow of JFK, for whom they applauded vigorously, it was La Callas who held their attention and won their adoration. At the first sound of her voice offstage singing, "Mario! Mario!" the audience held its breath. When she finally appeared she was greeted with a four-minute roar of applause. The performance ended at 11:40 that night, an hour after schedule: an entire hour of cheers and applause had been interspersed throughout the opera.

"I Started Dying When I Met This Man"

Through the next several months, Maria continued to drive herself until her doctors finally begged her to take a break. Her final appearance in an opera would be as Tosca at the Royal Gala in London on July 5th, 1965. She had no idea that it would be so at the time, of course, and Zeffirelli and she were discussing putting together a film version of *Tosca*. But as Zeffirelli put it, "Onassis realized that Maria was escaping from his clutches and, with diabolical shrewdness, convinced Maria to delegate him to finalize the contract. Everything went up in smoke, as he had planned." Little by little, desperation came to govern her relationship with Ari. Regardless of the affirmation she received from audiences, she continued to relinquish greater control of her life to him.

In 1966, Maria took an action that was, in many ways, a last attempt to force him into making a commitment to her: she relinquished her American citizenship and became a Greek citizen. With Meneghini she had "become" Italian, but at heart she always considered herself Greek. That she and Onassis could communicate in her "true" language was certainly a compelling factor in their relationship. By giving up her U.S. citizenship she was able to have her marriage to Meneghini, who had refused to divorce her, annulled and thereby remove the last official barrier in the way of a marriage to Ari. She was 43 and had discovered that she was pregnant; she hoped that this might convince Onassis finally to commit to her. When he found out about the pregnancy, he warned her that if she had the child it would be the end of their relationship.

His decision may have been made for dynastic reasons, but most likely it was because he was romancing one of the few women in the world more famous than Maria—Jacqueline Kennedy. Always someone to collect trophies, Onassis had pursued John F. Kennedy's lovely, young widow (whose physical similarities to Maria were remarkable), since the time of her husband's funeral. Unlike Maria, Jackie had the sort of fame that Onassis could relate to, compete with and add to. It was not based on something intangible like talent. Mrs. Kennedy had a brilliant pedigree and connections to one of the world's most powerful families. Wielding influence in Greece is nothing compared to having power in the United States.

Although she did not know at first whom he was seeing, Maria was aware that Ari was having an affair. Knowing how their own relationship had started, she could not have been surprised, and at first she seemed confident that their love was stronger than any flirtation he might take up on the side. Despite her desire to have a child, she agreed to have an abortion; perhaps this would make Onassis want to marry her. That he married Jackie Kennedy a mere eighteen months later indicates the extent to which Maria had been misguided. Although she had not permitted him to destroy her artistic career, she had allowed it to wither. She had little to show for her romantic devotion. As she tragically told mezzo-soprano Giulietta Simionato in 1968: "Giulia, remember my words. I started dying when I met this man and when I gave up my music."

Maria and Medea

Luckily for her, Maria's legend was so great that throughout these socially active but artistically fallow years, there were still many talented people interested in working with her. It was at this point in 1969 that Pasolini came forward and convinced her to make a film of *Medea*. It may have been that after so long away from serious study of her music and with an ever weakening, undependable voice, she was hesitant to return to the opera house. It may also have been that after years of talking about making a movie with Onassis the idea of conquering a new medium without his assistance was even more attractive. Whatever the reason, Pasolini had many of the characteristics she had grown comfortable with in her creative partners: he was gay, Communist, Italian, famous, and most importantly, gifted. He understood her aesthetic and was able to work in an intense, radical way that would allow her uniqueness to shine through. And he was interested in creating something that was, at least theoretically, for the masses.

Maria threw herself into the filming with the focus and will that had once been her trademarks. The story of Medea had suited her in the opera house partially because it was one of sacrifice, and Maria had been sacrificing her whole life. After nine years of fruitless pursuit of Ari, she understood this better than ever. "She was a semigoddess who put all her beliefs in a man," Maria said of Medea. "At the same time she is a woman with all the experiences of a woman, only bigger—bigger sacrifices, bigger hurts. She went through all these trying to survive. You can't put these things into words.... I began to look into the depths of Medea."

The movie was neither a critical nor popular success. Art house theaters and Callas fans appreciated it, but Pasolini had not quite made the Greek-epic, mass market film he'd strived for. Despite its lack of success, it did not cheapen her image. Working on the movie also inspired her to consider a return to singing.

By late 1970, after *Medea* was released, she was back in touch with Ari. He was one of those men who never quite allowed a relationship to end, even after he had moved on to another woman. Maria still loved him and despite the wisdom and advice of her friends, when he began to make overtures she did not rebuff them. It was not simply a matter of Onassis wanting two women—a man of his wealth and power could certainly have as many lovers as he wished—but he had realized that Jackie was not the ideal mate. The much-younger American's tastes did not mesh with his, and she was spending his money as if it was hers. It was about connecting: Maria and Ari were soulmates of a sort, while Ari and Jacqueline Kennedy Onassis clearly were not.

So whenever he was in Paris, where Maria had made her permanent home among the Parisians who had always worshipped her, they saw each other. This inspired in her the rebirth of the fantasy that they would eventually be married. If nothing else, the elation that came from this rekindling, combined with the limbering of her artistic muscles with *Medea*, convinced her to take on a series of master classes in Philadelphia and New York City. Through

1972, she led several, the most famous being at New York's Juilliard School. In them she shared her stage experience and offered insights into phrasing, characterization and acting. They offered a new view of her amazing artistry.

Comebacks

She also talked about comeback performances that never managed to come together. Towards this end, she was putting herself through a rigorous series of voice classes. During this period she and her old tenor-partner Giuseppe di Stefano renewed their friendship, and together they co-directed Verdi's *I vespri siciliani* at the Teatro Regio in Turin. Sadly, this effort revealed that a brilliant, inspired singer cannot necessarily translate that talent into directing. While she was working on *I vespri* word came to her that Ari's son, Alexander, had died in a plane crash. Several of his businesses were failing at the same time, and Ari was destroyed. He never recovered, mentally or physically. Seeing the emotional downfall of the man who had been both her tormentor and the great love of her life motivated her to revivify her own life.

After the mediocrity of the *I vespri* experience, Maria set out on a world tour with di Stefano. It was his idea, and as many critics have pointed out over the years, he risked little while she had everything to lose. As their friendship and working relationship were revived, and Ari declined before her, they also began a roman-

tic relationship. The tour began in Hamburg, Germany, in 1973, and ended a year later in Sapporo, Japan. It was supposed to be the comeback that admirers of "La Divina," as she was known, had been waiting more than a decade for, but Maria's voice was in shambles. Wear and tear, a lack of proper practice and re-training, emotional stress, lack of confidence, years of pushing the voice at both ends and giving too much to each performance—whatever the causes, she was a shadow of her former vocal self. Ultimately, few in the audience really cared. They wanted to see Callas and her mere presence created an uproar wherever she performed.

Endings

With the end of what would be her final tour came the end of her final romance. Maria knew early in the tour that the voice had, for the most part, left her. She did not accept this with equanimity, of course, but eventually she understood. She told Peter Diamond after a performance in London, "Don't tell me anything. I know. Go to Pippo. Tell him something, anything to pep him up." Di Stefano, who was still married and who had organized the first of these concerts as fund raisers for his ill daughter, was unsympathetic to her struggle and far too involved in his own. They parted on good terms, but Maria was left more unhappy than ever. She may have finally resigned herself to a life without the real love of a man and family, but the loss of her voice was insurmountable. Her words to journalist Peter Dragadze in a *Life* magazine interview in 1964 ring pathetically true: "Remember always that only a happy bird sings, while an unhappy one creeps into its nest and dies."

In 1975, Aristotle Onassis died after a gall bladder operation. His final years had been no happier than Maria's: he dealt with his son's death, divorced Jackie, and saw his empire collapse. Maria could not be at his side but she was able to monitor all of the details of his condition. She was shattered by his death.

On Friday, September 16, 1977, she died in the arms of her housekeeper in her Paris apartment. The official cause was "pulmonary thromboembolism," but there are many who think that she committed suicide. In her last year or so she had become addicted to pills, and as Meneghini said after her death, "Suicide? Maybe. But it is also possible that she killed herself unwittingly...by that continuous abuse of pills and various drugs. She was definitely a woman who no longer wanted to live."

Giuseppe di Stefano and Maria during her Farewell Tour of 1973. Although Maria clearly possessed only a shadow of the vocal powers that had made her famous, her dramatic sense was still intact, and fans were overjoyed to see her in person after a ten-year absence.

Maria outside of her home in Milan, 1976. By this time, she had become dependent upon an extensive regimen of pills, which was to contribute to her death in the following year.

Callas was able to exert control over everything in her professional life. She could perform when, where and what she wanted to, pick fights, and step on as many toes as she wished, because she was the real thing. But ultimately, she never seemed to be able to affect control over any of the deeper elements of her being: She had become a singer to attract the love and attention denied her by her mother; as she grew up she realized that she had both the talent and the determination to rise above all of her peers and be adored and respected by a huge public. In order to meet this destiny she set aside everything else in her life. Once she attained heights never before achieved by an opera singer, she realized that all she wanted were the things she had willed herself to set aside, and to return to them would have been to acknowledge that she had wasted her life. The result was that she was never able to get any of the "basic" things she desired, nor could she be happy with what she had earned. She told Giulietta Simionato in 1969, "In my life I have had some great successes, some great moments; but I was admired, not loved."

People who grew up listening to Elvis and the Beatles know the name of Maria Callas. In the contemporary world, where such "crossover" knowledge usually signifies a shallow under-standing, it is surprising how well, and how deeply, known she is a quarter century after her death. Her life may have been even larger than her greatest roles, but it was almost as sad as well. Her incandescence is in her art, and it is our great fortune that we can still hear it.

CHAPTER 2

The Art, the Tradition, the Voice

"The extraordinary success of Maria Callas appears, at first glance, one of the strangest phenomena in the world of performance of our time. Unique among sopranos, the reputation of this prodigious singer has crossed the limits normally set for even the most prestigious and great operatic artists. Other singers, of course, have succeeded in provoking enthusiastic reactions and even in unleashing passion, but this has always been within the relatively limited confines of opera lovers. The case of Callas is completely different. Her name today is familiar even to those who have no real contact with opera nor with the art of singing in general."

— RENÉ LIEBOWITZ

This quote from French conductor René Liebowitz (as recorded in Jean-Paul Sartre's journal *Les temps modernes*) is an interesting summation of the wonder that was Maria Callas. Her public persona was very public, indeed, moreso than any other opera singer of the twentieth century.

She got fired from the Metropolitan Opera; she dropped eighty pounds in one year, thereby transforming herself from ugly duckling to fashion icon; when asked about her mother, she once replied "She can go jump in the lake"; she walked out in the middle of a performance in Rome with the president of the republic in the audience; she demanded that colleagues she didn't like be fired and made what seemed like unreasonable demands on the general managers of opera houses in which she worked; she jet-setted around the globe; and she got infamously involved with—and jilted by—one of the richest men in the world.

As an artist, she was just as controversial. She was divisive and demanding, inspiring both ardent worshippers and scathing detractors. Many criticized the always problematic (or at least unreliable) metallic top of her voice or the somewhat stifled tone of her voice's middle and bottom. Others, hearing the same sounds, went wild with admiration for the colors of her tonal palette. Her sound actually angered some people—an unprecedented reaction in opera circles. But it is impossible to separate her voice from how she used it.

Range and Realities

As can be heard in recordings, the voice encompassed just under three octaves: In the Bolero from Verdi's *I vespri siciliani*, she touches on a low F-sharp and, in Rossini's *Armida*, a high F;

"Serafin once told me a marvelous thing. He said, 'You want to find out how the opera should be acted? You only have to listen to the music and you'll find everything there for you.' I seized on that immediately. I felt I knew exactly what he meant, and that is perhaps my biggest secret! I act according to the music — to a pause, to a chord, to a crescendo."

—MARIA CALLAS

both moments are brief and not particularly appealing, but even removing one note from each end, the range is impressive. There was lots of steel in the upper notes, an interesting, dark film over the middle-to-bottom, and an almost baritonal timbre to the bottom tones when she put pressure on them for dramatic effect. She pushed her chest register up to high G occasionally, which was exciting, but probably not particularly healthy. There was an odd resonance in her mouth, almost a buzz (sometimes described as a "bottled-up" sound), at mid-range; like it

Maria rehearses in her Ritz Hotel suite overlooking the Place Vendome, 1963. She performed a program of French and Italian arias at the Théâtre des Champs Elysées, receiving 15 curtain calls.

or not, it made her voice instantly recognizable—and if it was a flaw, she used it to her advantage. It was a voice of many colors and tones, ideal for expressing a vast range of emotions, and it combined strength and flexibility.

From the very start, the top notes could be unruly—a high D produced effortlessly and solidly one night might come out shrill or ragged three nights later. Moreover, she used three separate, rather than perfectly knit, voices for the top, middle and bottom of her range, and as thrilling and distinctive as that is, it must be seen as an imperfection. She often referred to her voice as an animal she couldn't tame, and try though she did, it would betray her. "The voice was answering tonight," she would say after a performance, or "the voice was not obeying tonight."

Sometime after 1955, for whatever reasons—singing roles that were too heavy or too high, leaning on the voice in a manner too muscular, an inherent flaw in the throat, the loss of a great deal of weight too quickly—a real, persistent problem began to emerge, and it remains the most controversial issue when discussing her voice. It began to appear on sustained notes above the G above the staff: a distinct fluctuation of the tone, a variation of the pitch, an undulation. It was not vibrato, which is a tool all singers (and some instrumentalists) use for expression, emphasis and, at, times, intensity and which implies a slight variance in tone. What Callas was producing was uncontrollable and was clearly not being done intentionally, for effect; it sounded, simply, wrong. As the fifties progressed, it became

more pronounced and, by 1960, it was frequently awful—a note left flapping in the wind, strident and outside of the correct pitch, which could wind up anywhere. Her detractors called it a "wobble;"; eventually, everyone did. But her technical equipment was fully in place: trills, scales, legato, embellishments were all within her command—she could make her voice do anything, most of the time, except sound plain and simply pretty. And control the wobble.

In a radio interview in the '60s, Callas said, "It is a matter of loving my kind of voice or not. Some people say I have a beautiful voice. Some people say I have not. It is a matter of opinion. Some people say I have a unique voice, and some people say it's just a whole big lie. That is also a matter of opinion. The only thing I can say is that people who don't like me can just not come and hear me. Because I—when I don't like something—I just don't bother about it."

And that, as they say, is that.

Predecessors and Protégés

In order to understand who she was as an artist, to find a precedent, one would have to go back to the early nineteenth-century singers Maria Malibran and Giuditta Pasta. These women were not simply known for their singing, they were great actresses (and vocal actresses), utterly convincing artists with, coincidentally, flawed voices. In addition, Callas's selfless dedication to the music and, within the music, to the story and

Maria Malibran (1808-1836), like Callas, was as appreciated for her acting as for her singing, and for her dedication to her work.

Bellini's Norma *and* La sonnambula, *as well as Donizetti's* Anna Bolena, *were written for Giuditta Pasta (1798-1865); they later became Callas staples.*

character, were, to believe contemporary reports, characteristics of Pasta's and Malibran's as well.

But historically, even before Pasta and Malibran, we must go back to the eighteenth century, a time when castrati—boys castrated right before puberty so that their voices remained high and agile even as they grew up to have the chest cavity, resonance and power of a man—were the greatest stars of opera, and when technically proficient singing was considered the height of excellence. The music was there to demonstrate the powers and glories of the voice—the breath control, evenness of tone, roulades, trills, leaps, ornaments. But by the nineteenth century, the church and common decency began eliminating the bizarre practice of castration,

and the female voice, which heretofore had been banned from the stage, came to prominence. As women were accepted as onstage performers, true drama, rather than a metaphor for true drama (i.e., a high male voice standing in for a woman's voice) began to take over. With this switch came Rossini, Donizetti and Bellini, composers who required plenty of vocal acrobatics, but sought a greater intermingling of vocalization, theater and emotion. This mixture was known as "bel canto," a complex term meaning literally "beautiful singing," but implying far more. Callas was practically single-handedly responsible, after close to a century of dormancy, for renewed interest in the operas of this period. Callas sang the aria *"Bel raggio"* from Rossini's arcane, florid, difficult *Armida* and Bellini's early *Il pirata* that brought these operas to the attention of current superstar soprano Renée Fleming.

Most of the great female voices of the time were naturally middle-ranged, but some began expanding their ranges upwards, without losing the bottom of their voices. Sopranos, indeed, all female singers, were expected to sing everything in the repertoire, but if they were famous enough, composers would write specifically for their particular talents. Giuditta Pasta's range was from low A to high D,

Gaetano Donizetti (1797-1848) around the time of the debut of his opera, Lucia di Lammermoor.

almost forgotten *Semiramide*; a few years later, it became a star vehicle for Joan Sutherland and Marilyn Horne. Donizetti's *Anna Bolena* was revived for Callas; by the '70s, Beverly Sills and Montserrat Caballé had re-discovered not only *Bolena*, but Donizetti's other pair of English-royalty operas, *Maria Stuarda* and *Roberto Devereux* as well. Similarly, Renata Scotto and Leyla Gencer based highlights of their careers on these operas. With the exception of Horne, who is a genuine mezzo and therefore unsuited, all of these women also sang Norma. And one can only presume that it was Callas's interest in Rossini's

The remarkable American coloratura soprano Beverly Sills as Norina in Donizetti's Don Pasquale. *The bel canto opera roles upon which Sills based much of her highly successful career are commonly felt to have been revived, almost singlehandedly, by Maria.*

Renata Scotto is among the great contemporary sopranos to make Bellini's Norma *a centerpiece of her repertoire, as Maria did.*

After the middle of the nineteenth century and into the early part of the twentieth, this sort of opera gave way to the music dramas of Wagner, later Verdi, and a genre of opera referred to as "verismo" (works that were "truth," or "reality" based), which were not compatible with the sort of vocal acrobatics and training that made up the essential arsenal of earlier singers. Rather, melodrama, volume and exclamation became more important, and the types of roles women sang, because of extreme demands and the growing size of orchestras and opera houses, began to be separated by vocal type: soprano, mezzo-soprano, contralto. Even sopranos were partitioned into "lyric," "coloratura" or "dramatic." She who sang Rossini did not sing late Verdi, Wagner or the Verists: Puccini, Leoncavallo, Giordano, et al.

with a particularly potent low register. Bellini wrote *Norma* and *La sonnambula* and Donizetti wrote *Anna Bolena*—pieces that would become Callas staples—for her. But Pasta's voice could be uneven and after a few seasons, she was known to stray wildly from pitch. Malibran, for whom Bellini revised *I puritani*, had a voice that naturally sat rather low, but she discovered a way to add an extension to it; the notes in the middle were occasionally called "dead spots." problems Callas's voice presented the same problems, and indeed, it has been suggested often that Callas was truly a mezzo-soprano whose training had given her an extra three or four notes.

Bringing Back Bel Canto

But Callas was a throwback; she could, and did, sing everything, and not only from the first half of the nineteenth century. Her very important and exhaustive training under Elvira de Hidalgo—herself a famous coloratura—was in the techniques of bel canto: Endless scales, divisions, rapid-fire runs, true legato, keeping the voice on the breath. But because her voice was ample and had an impressive edge to the top notes, she began her performing career by singing the so-called "dramatic" soprano repertoire. (Actually, in Greece, in her teens, she had sung Santuzza in *Cavalleria rusticana* and Leonore in *Fidelio*, roles requiring a darker timbre and often associated with mezzo-sopranos.) In 1948, her first full year as a professional

Maria's influential instructor Elvira de Hidalgo as Rosina in Il barbiere di Siviglia, *1916.*

singer (and the year in which the press began to notice her), she sang "big roles" such as Giocon-da, Leonora in Verdi's *La forza del destino*, Aida, Isolde, Turandot. By year's end, she had added Norma, which is not that strange for a dramat-ic soprano despite its reliance on bel canto technique, and it certainly did not indicate the direction she would soon take.

The turning point, and an accidental one it was at that, came early in 1949. Callas was singing the very heavy role of Brünnhilde in Wagner's *Die Walküre* under Tullio Serafin in Venice. Light coloratura soprano Margherita Carosio was singing Elvira in Bellini's then-infrequently performed *I puritani* on alternate evenings in the same opera house, and when Carosio backed out due to ill-ness, Serafin, who was conducting *Puritani* as well, found himself without an Elvira. Obviously hear-ing something very special in Callas's voice, he asked her to take over the part—a part that was in the domain of light, high voices. She learned it in eight days, between performances in *Die Walküre*, and triumphed. This changed every-thing: she sang with the intensity and fullness of a dramatic soprano but with the facility, felicity and all the notes of a Carosio type. The Venetian critic Mario Nordi wrote "A few days ago, a few were taken aback to read the name of a magnif-icent Brünnhilde, Isolde and Turandot announced in the role of Elvira. Last night everyone heard her and even the most skeptical had to admit that Maria Callas achieved a miracle."

She was twenty-five years old and had found her calling.

Renata Scotto in the title role of Lucia di Lammermoor, *1967.*

"She opened a door for us, for all the singers in the world, a door that had been closed. Behind it was sleeping not only great music but great ideas of interpretation. She has given us the chance, those who follow her, to do things that were hardly possible before her."

—MONTSERRAT CABALLÉ

And she knew what was good for her. Reminiscing to Harry Fleetwood, she stated, "By and by I started getting going and I sang Turandot all over Italy, hoping to God that I wouldn't wreck my voice. Because, you know, it's not really very good for the voice.... It's ruined quite a few voices. Well, you see, it's a rather nasty part, and it keeps on singing in a nervous way. And it taxes your vocal chords." And more pointedly, she told interviewer Edward Downes, "So I sang Isolde, then I sang Turandot also.... Then as soon as I could have gotten out of these roles, well I got out. In fact, I dedicated myself to the bel canto roles to do good for the voice, and I dropped all these other roles."

And in deciding to "do good for the voice," Callas started a mini-operatic revolution. The aesthetic principle behind these composers' specific notations—trills, ornaments, long-breathed phrases—had been to reinforce and amplify the dramatic situation being portrayed on stage. The phrase "bel canto" itself did not adhere until after its heyday, in the mid-nineteenth century, and although by then it implied "great art," it also suggested a certain shallowness of dramatic import. It was argued that the emphasis in bel canto was on vocal exhibitionism to indulge singers and their superficial audiences; the plots of the operas were seen to be empty-headed and predictable and the characters one-dimensional. And, in fact, by the mid-twentieth century, when the few bel canto operas still in the repertoire were performed, they *were* showcases for high-placed sopranos who could please the canary-fanciers in the audience, or, in the case of the comic operas of the time, they were a respite from the endless gloom and seriousness of Wagner, late Verdi and the Verists. They had, for the most part, become trite. Callas's interest in and eventual championing of the genre turned the critics and audiences on their heads and returned the art of bel canto to its original depth and aesthetic standards.

Dedication

Her commitment to her work was staggering: every recitative was as thought out as every aria at a time when sopranos in the so-called "light" roles sailed through the dramatic situations on their way to the next roulade and series of high notes. Mastering the recitatives requires an innate musicality and sense of dramatic context. Callas's performances became whole events, not just a series of arias and "moments." The public found her strange, initially disturbing, controversial. The conflict she created was between beauty on the one hand and expressiveness on the other.

Her repertoire grew and grew and her musical interests continued to expand. After she dropped Wagner, Aida and Turandot, she began adding roles—everything from Giordano's Fedora and Maddalena (in *Andrea Chénier*), to Puccini's Tosca and Butterfly, to all periods of Verdi, and, most importantly, for historical reasons, a dozen bel canto roles. She sang a bit of Mozart, *Die Entführung aus dem Serail* (in Italian translation), but it was perhaps the lack of overt emotionalism in his music that failed to whet her creative appetite. "I find most of Mozart's music dull," she said at a Juilliard master class in 1971. Disagree with her or not, her analysis of how to sing Mozart is worth noting: she told a student that Mozart's music is usually "sung with too much fragility. It should be sung with the same frankness you sing *Trovatore* with—but in a Mozart style."

She even tried her hand at comedy. In the Italian magazine, *Oggi*, she said "I accepted the offer from Maestro Cuccia to take part in a comic opera by Rossini, *Il turco in Italia*: a proposition which particularly appealed to

Maria begins a new, successful, but brief phase of her career, offering Master Classes at the Juilliard School of Music in New York, 1971.

me…because it allowed me to stray from the subject—by this time frequent—of great tragedies in music and to breathe the fresh air of a very funny Neapolitan adventure." It was an enormous success, unlike her portrayal of another comic Rossini heroine a year later, Rosina in *Il barbiere di Siviglia*. Even the conductor Carlo Maria Giulini (a great admirer of Callas's) was quoted as saying "Her personality was wrong, her conception misguided. She made Rosina a kind of Carmen…. I conducted every performance with my head down so I wouldn't see what was happening onstage." Her sound had little inherent levity in it, and it seems clear from letters and interviews with friends and contemporaries, that a sense of humor was not prominent among her attributes.

Nothing she sang wasn't a wonder of some kind: Rossini's *Armida* and Haydn's *Orfeo ed Euridice* dazzled with their virtuosity; Elena in

For the title role in Giordano's Fedora *(La Scala, 1956), Maria immersed herself in the Russian school of acting, which she studied with Tatiana Pavlova, herself an accomplished actress. She is seen here with the great tenor, Franco Corelli.*

Maria in a performance of Alceste, *in her first season at La Scala, 1953-1954. Director Luchino Visconti once suggested that her Greek heritage helped her to understand classical tragic characters and afford them the proper gravity.*

Verdi's *I vespri siciliani* showed off her strong gifts as a tragedienne. Even failures in such roles as Rosina and the relatively unimportant Fedora and Maddalena were very closely scrutinized, analyzed by the press and debated. Her Leonora in Verdi's *Il trovatore* was not the usual hand-to-forehead, one-dimensional character; she found the bel canto qualities in the role and

gnored none of the ornaments Verdi had composed and expected to be performed.

Her dips into sheer "classical" repertoire, like Gluck's *Alceste* and *Iphigénie en Tauride* and Spontini's *La Vestale*, might not pass muster with today's historically correct attitudes towards such works, but she gave their heroines the stature and formality they required, and, in a way, removed

Maria as Anna Bolena *at La Scala, 1957.*

them from their peculiar perch on the sidelines of performed operas. (Director Luchino Visconti suggested that her Greek background helped her understand these Classical characters.)

Her *Madama Butterfly* and Gilda in *Rigoletto* exhibited an innocence and girlishness—not just in her demeanor, but in her ability to lighten her tone—which surprised those who saw her as the epitome of womanhood. Less filled with insights (but nonetheless thrilling) was her Aida, a role that lacks the contrasts Callas seemed to relate to instinctively, but her performances of the role were still wildly applauded; of her Elisabetta in *Don Carlo* (a role she sang only a handful of times), a critic wrote that she "lacks the sweetness and softness necessary in moments of abandon…." but recordings of the character's last act aria made after she had dropped the role from her repertoire are impressive on every level except the sheerly vocal. Her Amelia in *Un ballo in maschera* was a triumph; she epitomized the woman's desperation.

Her performances of Donizetti's almost-forgotten *Anna Bolena* in 1957 were pivotal; they are acknowledged to be the start of the bel canto revival. Callas had an affinity for Anna, finding the innocence in this wronged, melancholy character. "Now history has its Anna Bolena, which is quite different from Donizetti's," she is quoted as saying. "Donizetti made her a sublime woman, a victim of circumstance, nearly a heroine. I couldn't bother with history's story; it really ruined my insight. I had to go by the music, by the libretto." With her understanding

of Anna's blamelessness, her anger and her haughtiness, combined with spectacular vocalism (from low A to high D, *à la* Pasta), she turned what was thought to be a dead, historical opera into a high drama that drove audiences to their feet.

As Amina in Bellini's *La sonnambula* (particularly at La Scala under Leonard Bernstein), she once again transformed a work with a dim-witted plot into something people could care about. She perfectly captured the character's tender nature while hardly stinting on her unbridled passion in the final scene, and the delicacy of her physical acting was compared to the work of a ballerina. The same might be said of her Elvira in *I puritani*, a one-dimensional character to which, in addition to the requisite razzle-dazzle, she brought a type of melancholy that summarized Bellini's appeal.

Late in her career, in relatively poor voice, she added Bellini's Imogene in *Il pirata* and Donizetti's Paolina in *Poliuto*—operas which had been all but forgotten—and made the characters come vividly to life despite her sometimes severe vocal shortcomings.

Certain roles are, to this day, inextricably associated with Callas: Any soprano who tries any of them since is instantly compared with her. They are Donizetti's Lucia di Lammermoor, Verdi's Violetta and Lady Macbeth, Tosca, Cherubini's Medea, and Bellini's heroines in *I puritani* and *La sonnambula*, and most importantly, Norma. Luckily, we have some of her thoughts on these roles, all in her strangely constructed English.

"Absolutely Sure"

Her Lucia caused a revolution. At the opera's premiere in 1835, members of the audience wept audibly when the heroine went mad; by the 1930s and '40s, light, chirpy sopranos interested only in high notes, staccati and "effects" (Lily Pons and Toti dal Monte come to mind) had taken over the role, with the public's approval. She understood what effect the opera was supposed to have and returned the drama, sadness and urgency to the part while hardly ignoring its musically athletic, canary-fancying qualities.

"Very sure, the first Mexico performance [of Lucia]," she told Edward Downes in a 1967

Maria giving an acclaimed performance of Lucia di Lammermoor, *Chicago 1954.*

radio broadcast. "Absolutely sure, beautiful top notes and all that, *but it was not yet the role.* Of course, it was lovely. I remind you that Lucia was the same soprano that used to sing Norma and *Pirata* and *Sonnambula.* So you see, it's not a light role. It is a dramatico-coloratura. In fact, Lucia is a very low role and light sopranos have to put the third act high, because it's terribly centrale, as they say." And to Kenneth Harris, in a February 1970 *Observer* review: "I dislike violence, and I find it artistically inefficient. Where is it necessary to include the shedding of blood? The suggestion of the action is more moving than the exhibition of it. I always eliminated the knife when singing Lucia: I thought it was a useless and old-fashioned business, that the action could get in the way of the art and realism interfere with the truth."

Of Cherubini's child-murdering Medea, she told Derek Prouse in the London *Sunday Times* (in March 1961): "This opera is not bel canto but recitative and theatre—straight acting, speaking with the music. The strength of Cherubini's opera is not the arias but the recitativi.... The way I saw Medea was the way I feel it: fiery, apparently calm but very intense. The happy time with Jason is now past; now she is devoured by misery and fury."

And she made this remarkable confession in a 1967 Met broadcast interview: "I was doing Medea then and ... my first instinct was saying that the face is too fat and I can't stand it. Because I needed the chin for expression in certain very hard phrases and cruel phrases, or tense phrases

Medea _at the Dallas Civic Opera House, 1958. Maria's weight early in her career was an embarrassment to her, and she explained later, after she'd shed the excess pounds, that she needed defined, dramatic facial and neck lines to portray the role properly._

And I felt, as a woman of the theater that I was and am that I needed these neck lines and the chin lines to be very thin and very pronounced. So I was annoyed, I darkened the color and all that, but it's nonsense. You can't DO that...And then I was tired of playing a game like, for instance, playing a beautiful young woman and I was a heavy, uncomfortable woman to move around....And I felt, now, if I'm going to do things right—I studied all my life to put things right musically—why don't I just diet and put myself into a certain condition [so] that I'm presentable?"

She was the world's great Violetta in _La traviata_, and she sang the role more often than any besides Norma. She told _Life_ magazine that she

Maria and Giuseppe di Stefano in La traviata, *La Scala, 1955. Director Luchino Visconti declared that he had staged this production "only for [Maria], not for myself. I did it to serve Callas, for one must serve a Callas."*

saw the role "and therefore the voice, as fragile, weak and delicate. It is a trapeze part filled with sick pianissimo," and elaborated, once again to Derek Prouse, in 1961: "I had strived for years to create a sickly quality in the voice for Violetta; after all, she is a sick woman. It's all a question of breath, and you need a very clear throat to sustain this tired way of talking, or singing, in

round tones? It would be ridiculous. And in the last act they even said, 'Callas is having trouble with her breath.' Thank Heaven I eventually attained what I was trying to do and got the proof that I had been appreciated."

This comment from director Franco Zeffirelli tells us much about Callas: "I begged Maria to be prudent, to avoid unreasonable vocal challenges. But she refused, saying 'I can't, Franco. I won't do what Anna Moffo does in _Traviata_. I won't skim through my music. I have to take chances, even if it means a disaster and the end of my career. I must try for all the notes, even if I miss some.'

Her five live performances of Lady Macbeth were legendary. She infused the complex, wicked character with knowing nuance and her sleep

this case. And what did they say? 'Callas is tired. The voice is tired.' But that was precisely the impression I was trying to create. How could Violetta be in her condition and sing in big,

Maria as Violetta at the Palacio de Bellas Artes, 1951.

Maria and Mario Del Monaco introduce the 1955-1956 La Scala season with a triumphant performance of Norma.

walking scene was both pitiable and terrifying. "The voice should be heavy, thick and strong," she told *Life* magazine. "The role, and therefore the voice, should have an atmosphere of darkness."

"It Is Not Enough to Have a Beautiful Voice"

Her dislike for the role of Tosca was well known, but it was the role in which she reconquered the Metropolitan Opera in 1965, after an absence of several years. The 6,500 tickets (for which there had been close to 50,000 requests) had to be stored in a safe. People lined up four days in advance for standing room tickets. Leonard Bernstein, Bette Davis, and Robert, John and (ironically) Jacqueline Kennedy were among the celebrities at the first of the two performances.

Again, to Edward Downes: "Well, [Tosca] is not that beautiful, frankly, because the first act is just a nervous girl that is always complaining. And the second act automatically goes on its own, with the '*Vissi d'arte*,' which I think should be cut out eventually because it stops completely the action of the second act. In fact, I was pleased to hear that [even] Puccini didn't want it ... you can feel it, it just stops the movement."

Fortunately, there are two commercial (and several private) recordings of the opera and two videos of her second act that confirm her ability to transcend her aversion to a role.

But if there is one role for which she will be remembered, it is Norma. It is a demanding role, emotionally wrenching, and she is onstage for three-quarters of the opera. Vocally it is no less taxing: soprano Lilli Lehmann claimed it was harder than Brünnhilde. "Norma resembles me in a certain way," Callas once said. "She seems very strong and ferocious at times. Actually, she is not, even though she roars like a lion." "With an opera like Bellini's *Norma*... [Callas to Jay Harrison of *New York Herald*, October 28, 1956, before her Met premiere in the role] I work as though I had never sung it before. It is the most difficult role in my repertory; the more you do it, the less you want to." And "...maybe she's something like my own character: the grumbling woman who is very proud to show her real feelings and proves at the end exactly what she is. She is a woman who cannot be nasty or unjust in a situation for which she herself is fundamentally to blame." (Callas to London *Sunday Times*, March 27, 1961)

In an interview late in her career, again, in her own peculiarly inflected English, Callas summed up her views on what she did for a living: "Bel canto does not mean beautiful singing alone. It is, rather, the technique demanded by the composers of this style—Donizetti, Rossini and Bellini. It is the same attitudes and demands of Mozart and Beethoven, for example, the same approach and the same technical difficulties faced by instrumentalists. You see, a musician is a musician. A singer is no different from an instrumentalist except that we have words. You don't excuse things in a singer you would not dream of excusing in a violinist or pianist. There is no excuse for not having a trill, in not doing the *acciaccatura*, in not having good scales. Look at your scores! There are technical things written there to be performed, and they must be performed whether you like it or not. How will you get out of a trill? How will you get out of scales when they are written there, staring you in the face? It is not enough to have a beautiful voice. What does that mean? When you interpret a role, you have a thousand colors to portray happiness, joy, sorrow, fear. How can you do this with only a beautiful voice? Even if you sing harshly sometimes, as I have frequently done, it is a necessity of expression. You have to do it, even if people will not understand. But in the long run they will, because you must persuade them of what you are doing."

According to her most important teacher, Elvira de Hidalgo, to whom Callas referred frequently with something akin to reverence: "Maria abused her God-given gifts." And, indeed, she sang everything she wanted to, in the manner she thought most appropriate to the character

Maria in 1976.

and her music, and probably drove her voice into premature decline. Conductor Nicola Rescigno, who led her American debut in Chicago, said that what set Callas apart from everyone else was her "willpower." Her "prime" is considered to have lasted only a decade, but she continued—and continues—to change the way people listen to opera. To this day, when opera lovers and other singers discuss the way opera is perceived and what is expected of a singer, they often refer to B.C. and A.C.—Before and After Callas. One has only to hear her to understand why.

CALLAS SPEAKS

On Tosca: *"Tosca is not that beautiful, frankly, because the first act is just a nervous girl that is always complaining. And the second act automatically goes on its own, with the "Vissi d'arte," which I think should be cut out eventually because it stops completely the action of the second act. In fact, I was pleased to hear that [even] Puccini didn't want it…you can feel it, it just stops the movement."*—Interview with Edward Downes, 1967

On Turandot: *"I sang Turandot all over Italy, hoping to God that I wouldn't wreck my voice. Because, you know, it's not really good for the voice…It's ruined quite a few voices. Well, you see, it's a rather nasty part, and it keeps on singing in a nervous way. And it taxes your vocal chords."* —Interview with Harry Fleetwood

On Norma: *"It is the most difficult role in my repertory; the more you do it, the less you want to."* —To Jay Harrison of The New York Herald, *Oct. 28, 1956, before her Metropolitan Opera premiere in the role*

"Maybe she's something like my own character: the grumbling woman who is very proud to show her real feelings and proves at the end exactly what she is. She is a woman who cannot be nasty or unjust in a situation for which she herself is fundamentally to blame." —To London Sunday Times, *March 27, 1961*

On La Traviata: *"I had strived for years to create a sickly quality in the voice for Violetta; after all, she is a sick woman. It's all a question of breath, and you need a very clear throat to sustain this tired way of talking, or singing, in this case. And what did they say? 'Callas is tired. The voice is tired.'… And in the last act they even said, 'Callas is having trouble with her breath.' Thank Heaven I eventually attained what I was trying to do and got the proof that I had been appreciated."* —Interview with Derek Prouse, London Sunday Times, *March 19, 1961*

On Lucia di Lammermoor: *"I dislike violence and I find it artistically inefficient. Where is it necessary to include the shedding of blood? The suggestion of the action is more moving than the exhibition of it. I always eliminated the knife when singing Lucia: I thought it was a useless and old-fashioned business, that the action could get in the way of the art, and realism interfere with the truth."* —To Kenneth Harris, Observer Review, *February 8, 1970*

On Medea: *"This opera is not bel canto but recitative and theatre—straight acting, speaking with the music. The strength of Cherubini's opera is not the arias but the recitative…and if we had done it in the classical style we could never have brought it to life: There would have been no fire to it. The way I saw Medea was the way I feel it: Fiery, apparently calm but very intense. The happy time with Jason is now past; now she is devoured by misery and fury."* —Callas to Derek Prouse, London Sunday Times, *March 19, 1961*

The Performances of Maria Callas

Even those who know little about Maria Callas know that she was a great actress as well as a singer—a rarity on the opera stage. But since her stage performances were very few toward the end of her life, in the 1960s, most opera lovers, and most of her current great admirers, actually never saw her perform. The few extant videotapes are impressive indeed, and even in still photographs, her vibrancy, ability to communicate, and passion come through.

But her fame and position are kept alive mainly by her recordings, and rightly so. The remarkable thing about them is that they do *not* present an incomplete picture of her art; she was, first and foremost an opera *singer*. Through the sounds she made, her identification with the character and the music, she could draw a complete portrait of that human being in a matter of moments. She could seduce, upset and anger the listener; you might worry

Maria in Spontini's La Vestale, La Scala, 1954.   133

for her or share in her joy. Some voices, due to their heft or hue, are not naturally suited to certain roles; Callas managed, time after time, to overcome any limitations when a role interested her. "When you interpret a role," Callas said, "you have to have a thousand colors to portray happiness, joy, sorrow, fear. How can you do this with only a beautiful voice?" Keep that in mind—the concept of "a thousand colors"—while you listen to the many characters portrayed on these disks by one woman.

Some of the arias here are inextricably linked to Callas, others she sang a few times, a handful represent the French mezzo-soprano repertoire which came to interest her after 1961, and a few are just pieces she opted to record for the sake of leaving her imprint on them. They come from the years 1954-64; some show her at peak form, without a vocal blemish, some are clearly the work of a voice in decline. With a rare exception or two, none exhibit an artist giving anything less than her best; even performances unappealing to the ear contain moments in which she conveys something worth noting in a character that a finer, smoother vocalist might have no idea how to convey. Words are shaded in ways that define singing; if the spoken word could communicate what Callas expresses with tonal nuance, there would be no reason to listen to singing.

For most of the selections, I've pointed out specific touches that listeners new to Callas (and even some who are familiar with her) may not otherwise notice; for a few, the aria as a whole needs little explanation. Her charisma may have come, in part, from her physical presence, but most of it came from her voice. Those who feel that because they never saw her in the flesh, they missed the Callas phenomenon, are wrong. All you have to do to "get" Callas, to understand who she was and what she did for (and to) the music she performed—and opera in general—is to *listen*.

Compact Disc 1

TRACK 1: BELLINI *CASTA DIVA (NORMA)*

NORMA e MINISTRE
Casta Diva, che inargenti,
Queste sacre antiche piante,
A noi volgi il bel sembiante
Senza nube e senza vel...

NORMA and PRIESTESSES
chaste goddess, who dost bathe in silver
these ancient, hallowed trees,
turn thy fair face upon us,
unveiled and unclouded...

German soprano Christa Ludwig and Maria working on the definitive 1960 recording of Norma, *London.*

Tempra, o Diva, tempra tu de' cori ardenti,
Tempra ancora Io zelo audace,
Spargi in terra quella pace
Che regnar tu fai nel ciel…

Temper thou the burning hearts,
the excessive zeal of thy people,
enfold the earth in that sweet peace
which, through thee, reigns in Heaven…

Vincenzo Bellini (1801–35) is one of the triumverate of composers, along with Gioacchino Rossini and Gaetano Donizetti, who epitomized the age of bel canto. Bel canto is a term used often throughout this book, and while it is easily, literally defined as "beautiful singing," it is far more than that. The term implies not only a beauty of tone but an expertise in all aspects of singing: breath control, portamento, legato, to name three. "Bel canto" encompasses a type of overt emotionalism which nevertheless must never mar the sung line, and a concentration on melody in conjunction with vocal prowess to communicate and define character. Bellini's seductive, melancholy, endless melodies work simply, and he tried, throughout his career, to mix music and text so carefully that they became one.

Norma was the eighth of the ten operas he composed in his short life, and is generally considered his masterpiece. The title role, in addition to being the apotheosis of bel canto, is also among the most difficult, musically and dramatically, ever written.

This is the role Callas sang on stage more than any other—more than 90 times between 1948 and 1965. Norma's complex loyalties, her nobility, her shame, her rage and her eventual sacrifice suited Callas's sense of tragedy and drama, both personal and professional.

The opera takes place in first-century Gaul. Norma, high priestess of the Druids, wishes, unlike her father Oroveso and many others in the community, to avoid war with the Romans. Her reasons are personal: unbeknownst to her people she loves the Roman Proconsul and has borne him two children. "*Casta diva*" ("Chaste goddess") is her noble entrance aria in the first act; as the High Priestess she leads her people in a hymn to the moon goddess. (All ends badly, with Norma and her lover being sacrificed at the opera's close, and the children placed in her father's care.)

Despite Callas's less-than-perfect vocal state (this was recorded late in 1960) this is a fine, properly hypnotic reading, and is, in fact, a good example of how unimportant a poorly produced note or two can be within the framework of an entire aria. In a way, "*Casta diva*" illustrates Callas vocally: perfection and dazzling effects in one minute, rough, troublesome tone in the next.

The opening phrases are smoothly sung, with a fine diminishing of the tone at the end of each one (0:35; 0:58): Callas never loses sight that this is an invocation coming from a real believer. The lifts to the repeated high As and final

B-flat (from 1:19) are rapturous. The "little notes" in the melismatic middle section (2:05 ff) bubble naturally and elegantly, and the three descending figures starting at 2:37 are as graceful as water droplets. The second verse (at 3:00) is just as lovely but more urgent, as the text, which asks the Goddess to "temper the excessive zeal of her people," becomes stronger. The repeated high notes may not be beautiful, but they evoke the passion of the moment, and the cadenza at the end (starting at 4:54) lands on a big, nasty high B-flat, off which Callas flows as peacefully and artfully as a waterfall: its not for nothing that this type of descending vocal line was called, throughout her career, the "Callas string of pearls."

Maria receiving an ovation at the close of a recital at the Civic Opera House, Chicago, 1958.

TRACK 2: CATALANI
EBBEN?... NE ANDRÒ LONTANA (LA WALLY)

WALLY	WALLY
Ebben? Ne andrò lontana,	Well? I shall go far away,
come va l'eco della pia campana…	As far as the echo of the hallowed bell…
là, fra la neve bianca!	Up there amid the white snows,
là, fra le nubi d'or!	Up there amid the golden clouds,
laddove la speranza, la speranza,	Where hope is
è rimpianto, è rimpianto, è dolor!	Regret and sorrow!
O della madre mia casa gioconda,	O pleasant house of my mother,
la Wally ne andrà da te, da te lontana assai,	Wally is going far, far away from you,
e forse a te, e forse a te non farà mai più ritorno,	And maybe will never more return to you,
ne più la rivedrai!	And you will never see her again!
Mai più…mai più…	Never again…never again…
Ne andrò sola e lontana	I will go far away, alone
come l'eco della pia campana,	like the echo of the hallowed bell,
là, fra la neve bianca!	up there amid the white snows:
n'andrò, n'andrò sola e lontana…	I'll go alone and far away
e fra le nubi d'or!	up among the golden clouds!

Alfredo Catalani (1854–93) was a distinguished composer whose career was cut short by an early death. His opera *La Wally*, now almost forgotten except for the aria recorded here, is his finest; indeed, the great conductor Arturo Toscanini thought well enough of it to name his daughter Wally after its heroine.

The opera takes place in the Tyrolean Alps. In this aria, Wally has been ordered out of the house by her father because she refuses to marry the man he has chosen for her. In her sad state, she imagines herself far from home, alone in the snowy mountains. (A note: The man Wally does, in fact, love dies in an avalanche in the final scene—a unique operatic plot turn.) As noted, the opera is rarely performed and Callas never sang the role on stage, but when she recorded it here for a recital, she was at her vocal peak.

In the opening moments, the orchestra depicts the bleak, windswept landscape. Callas as Wally enters (0:53), resolute but sad, dreamily picturing the snow and clouds in which she's about to find herself adrift. The voice hardens and then pulls back with the realization that the only possibility in this climate is regret and sorrow; the darkening of the tone towards and on the word "*dolor*" – "sorrow" (1:56-2:07) is typical of the type of vocal word-painting Callas is rightly famous for. When Wally's thoughts turn to her mother and past happiness (2:25) the sound softens sweetly, but the real possibility that she might never see her again (3:00) brings back the feel- ing of desolation. On "*Mai più*" – "Never again" (3:28-3:41), she draws the note to a whisper, almost unable to imagine such a situation. The first thoughts and words return, and as the sense of sadness returns with them, the truth of the situation dawns, and Callas rises to a blazing, solid high B-natural, ending the aria on a fierce and tragic note.

TRACK 3: PUCCINI
O MIO BABBINO CARO (GIANNI SCHICCHI)

LAURETTA	LAURETTA
O mio babbino caro,	Oh, dear daddy,
mi piace, è bello bello;	I love him, he's so handsome;
vo' andare in Porta Rossa	I want to go to Porta Rossa
a comperar l'anello!	to buy the ring!
Sì, sì ci voglio andare!	Yes, yes, I mean it.
E se l'amassi indarno,	And if my love were in vain,
andrei sul Ponte Vecchio,	I'd go to the Ponte Vecchio
ma per buttarmi in Arno!	and throw myself in the Arno!
Mi struggo e mi tormento!	I fret and suffer torments!
O Dio, vorrei morir!	O God, I'd rather die!
Babbo, pietà, pietà!	Daddy, have pity!
Babbo, pietà, pietà!	Have pity, I implore you!

Giacomo Puccini (1858–1924) is one of the greatest and best-known composers of Italian opera. Situations in his operas are dramatically charged, melodies are bountiful and memorable, and his ability to wring an emotion out of an audience verges on the manipulative—not altogether a bad combination.

Gianni Schicchi is part of a trilogy of one-act operas known as *Il trittico*, which had their premiere at New York's Metropolitan Opera

Maria at the height of her career, circa 1957.

House in 1918. It is Puccini's only comedy. The plot, taken from Dante's *Divine Comedy*, concerns greedy relatives who gather around the deathbed of their wealthy uncle; when they discover that he's left everything to a monastery, they ask Gianni Schicchi, an old trickster, to crawl into the deathbed, call a notary, and change "his" will in their favor. Schicchi's daughter Lauretta is in love with the dead man's nephew, and in this aria she begs her father's permission to marry him. As it turns out, Schicchi does trick the notary, but he leaves the house to Lauretta and her boyfriend, and everything else to his "good friend, Gianni Schicchi."

One couldn't ask for a greater contrast of character or sound from Wally than Lauretta. (Note that the two were recorded at the same sessions in September of 1954.) Lauretta is a loved, coy, privileged, lighthearted youngster. Callas was rarely girlish or lighthearted—these are traits that she rarely exhibited in her private or public life—so it's remarkable how she manages to convince. Lauretta is another part she never played onstage, but she included this aria in her recitals late in her career. It's not vocally challenging, and its easy, memorable tune accounts for its popularity.

Callas is self-consciously girlish here—small, light, demure—Lauretta knows how to get what she wants from her "dear dad" – "*babbino caro*." The tone remains the same until she threatens to throw herself in the Arno – "*ma per buttarmi in Arno*" (1:16), with a slight pout on the word "*buttarmi*" – "throw myself." She's snuggling up to him

and continues to do so while she melodramatically sings "*O Dio, vorrei morir*" – "O God, I want to die" (1:35 ff). Lauretta's youthfully theatrical behavior is adorable, and Callas understands just how to entice. Frankly, her tone is too mature for the character (whom I'm sure she'd never give a second thought to), but even given that, she does wonders with the situation.

Maria as Maddalena in Andrea Chénier *at La Scala, 1954.*

TRACK 4: GIORDANO
LA MAMMA MORTA (ANDREA CHÉNIER)

MADDALENA

La mamma morta
m'hanno alla porta
della stanza mia;
moriva e mi salvava!
Poi a notte alta io con Bersi errava,
quando ad un tratto, un livido bagliore
guizza e rischiara innanzi a' passi miei
la cupa via!
Guardo…Bruciava il loco di mia culla!

Così fui sola!…E intorno il nulla!

Fame e miseria…
Il bisogno, il periglio…
Caddi malata!
E Bersi, buona e pura,
di sua bellezza ha fatto
un mercato, un contratto per me!
Porto sventura a chi bene mi vuole!

Fu in quel dolore
che a me venne l'amor!
voce piena d'armonia,
e dice:"Vivi ancora! Io son la vita!"
Ne' miei occhi è il tuo cielo!
Tu non sei sola! Le lagrime tue
io le raccolgo! Io sto sul tuo cammino
e ti sorreggo!

MADDELENA

They killed my mother
at the door
of my room;
she died — she saved me!
Then late at night I was straying with Bersi
when, all of a sudden, a livid flash
flickers and lights, before my steps,
the dark path!
I looked…the place that cradled me was
     burning!

So I was alone!… and around me
     nothingness!…
hunger and poverty…
need, danger…
I fell ill!
And good, pure Bersi
sold her beauty,
bargained it away, for me!
I bring misfortune to those who love me!

It was during that sorrow
that love came to me! —
a voice filled with harmony —
and said: "Live still! I am Life
Thy heaven is in my eyes!
Thou art not alone! I gather
thy tears! I walk along thy path
and sustain thee!

Sorridi e spera! Io son l'amore!	Smile and hope! I am Love!
Tutto intorno è sangue e fango?	Is everything around thee blood and mud?
Io son divino!	I am divine!
Io son l'oblìo…	I am Oblivion…
Io son il dio	I am the god
che sovra il mondo scenda dall'empireo	that descends from the heaven to earth
fa della terra il ciel…	and makes of earth a heaven…
Ah! Io son l'amore!"	Ah! I am Love!"

Umberto Giordano (1867–1948) composed 12 operas, out of which only *Andrea Chénier* has found a place in the permanent repertory. Although Giordano can never be accused of genius, *Andrea Chénier*, filled with verismo-style dark passions, violence and gritty situations, nonetheless contains some thrilling music which never fails to move an audience.

Callas sang Madeleine de Coigny only six times, all at La Scala, in Milan, during a one-month period in 1955. The role is brief and of secondary importance to that of the tenor, Chénier. The character is one-dimensional, hardly the obvious choice for a complex, star soprano, and her performances of it were not particularly memorable.

Set in Paris immediately before and during the French Revolution, the opera's focal point is the idealist and poet Andrea Chénier. At this moment in the opera's third act, Chénier has been condemned to death. The former aristocrat Madeleine de Coigny, who has fallen in love with Chénier and his ideals, comes before the tribunal and pleads for his life. In this aria, sung to the revolutionary leader Gerard who used to be her servant, she describes with horror how she saw her mother die in the flames which devoured her home, a fire set by an angry mob. In utter despair, fearful, hungry, poor and ill, Love came to her—and it was only Love that gave her the will to continue living. (At the opera's close, Madeleine takes the place of another woman and goes triumphantly to the guillotine with Chénier.)

In superb voice throughout (this was recorded in '54 as well), Callas gets everything available out of this aria, even managing to make sense of the fact that half the words are supposedly uttered by the idealized figure of Love. A sad cello melody introduces the mood and Callas, in the opening words ("They killed my mother at the door of my room"), is as dark as dark can be (0:56 ff), using a tone which is close to emotionless, as befits the character's catatonic dejection. But as she conjures the image of the flames surrounding her, the panic in her voice is palpable, then settles back into the deadness of loneliness and illness. She's gentle when thinking of her maid Bersi's sacrifice (2:00 ff). And then, as if in a dream (2:35 ff), she recounts how Love came to her. At that point, as if transported—which is, after all, what the aria is about—she continues through to the end with solid tone and true enthusiasm, even managing to sing the lines "I am divine, I am oblivion" (4:00–4:11) without sounding deranged. She continues upward and onward in a growing hallucinatory frenzy to a stunning high B with the realization that (paraphrased) love is all you need. The aria's overt mania and emotionalism make it work; in essence, it's a piece of melodramatic junk that almost never fails on stage. Callas transcends its trashiness—almost.

TRACK 5: PUCCINI *VISSI D'ARTE (TOSCA)*

TOSCA

Vissi d'arte, vissi d'amore,
non feci mai male ad anima viva!…
Con man furtiva
quante miserie conobbi, aiutai…
Sempre con fè sincera,
la mia preghiera
ai santi tabernacoli salì.
Sempre con fè sincera,
diedi fiori agl' altar.
Nell'ora del dolore perchè
perchè Signore, perchè
me ne rimuneri così?…
Diedi gioielli
della Madonna al manto,
e diedi il canto agli astri,
al ciel, che ne ridean più belli.
Nell'ora del dolore perchè,
perchè, Signore,
perchè me ne rimuneri così?

TOSCA

I lived for art, I lived for love:
Never did I harm a living creature!…
Whatever misfortunes I encountered
I sought with secret hand to succour…
Ever in pure faith,
my prayers rose
in the holy chapels.
Ever in pure faith,
I brought flowers to the altars.
in this hour of pain. Why,
why, Oh Lord, why
dost Thou repay me thus?
Jewels I brought
for the Madonna's mantle,
and songs for the stars in heaven
that they shone forth with greater radiance.
In this hour of distress, why,
why, Oh Lord,
why dost Thou repay me thus?

The story of *Tosca* was taken from a well-known, successful, highly sensational play of the same name which had become famous as a vehicle for the actress Sarah Bernhardt. Another composer, Alberto Franchetti, had already secured the rights to it when Puccini became interested in it, but Puccini and his publisher, Ricordi, managed to convince Franchetti that it was unworkable as an opera, and he gave up the rights. The next day, Puccini took them over. His instincts (if not his morals or methods), as usual, were right, and the opera was a popular success at its premiere in Rome despite the press's horror with its tawdry, shocking plot. To this day, *Tosca* has never fallen out of favor with audiences and sopranos alike.

Tosca's lover, Mario Cavaradossi, is about to be executed at the order of the evil Chief of Police, Baron Scarpia, who lusts after Tosca. Scarpia has just told Tosca that Mario will go free after a mock execution, if he, Scarpia, can have his way with her. Here, Tosca, a religious woman, stops and sings the aria *"Vissi d'arte"* –

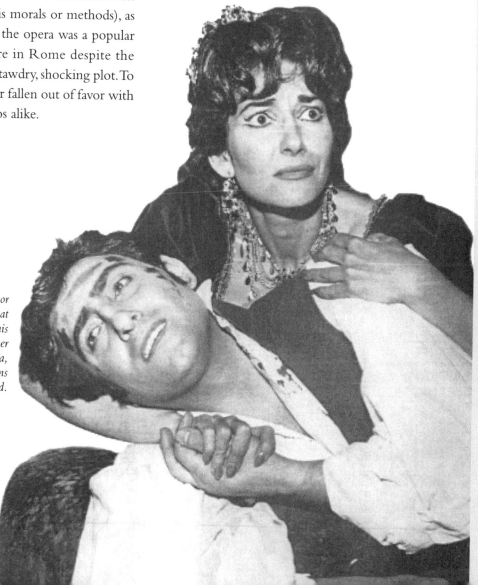

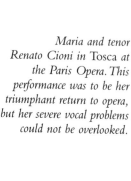

Maria and tenor Renato Cioni in Tosca at the Paris Opera. This performance was to be her triumphant return to opera, but her severe vocal problems could not be overlooked.

"I have lived for art," in which she desperately questions God as to how He could possibly punish her so. After the aria, when Scarpia lunges at Tosca, she stabs him to death and races to the mock execution. It turns out to be a real execution, Cavaradossi is killed, and as the authorities, who have by now discovered the murder of Scarpia, come to capture Tosca, she leaps from the top of the building to her death.

Callas's relationship with *Tosca* began in 1941 or 1942 in Athens (sung in Greek) and ended in London in 1965 as her final performance in a staged opera. She claimed to dislike the work, telling interviewer Edward Downes that in "…the first act [she] is a nervous girl that is always complaining," and that the great centerpiece aria in the second act, recorded here, "should be cut out…because it stops completely the action." Nonetheless, she sang it successfully almost 40 times and recorded it twice, and it is considered one of her most thrilling portrayals. This is taken from her 1953 complete recording of the opera, to this day considered the ideal by which other recordings of *Tosca* must be judged.

There is plenty in this very famous aria for Callas to sink her interpretive teeth into. She underplays the melodrama and thereby makes the drama more effective, never losing sight of the fact that Tosca is very religious. The opening phrases are delivered with emotional exhaustion and misunderstanding at her plight. This passage is followed by a brief outburst when she thinks about her misfortunes but she stifles herself, realizing that she should be praying, not complaining. From 0:56 to 2:00 she expresses her lifelong faith in ultimately sad, still-penitent tones, beginning to wonder why she is being repaid so cruelly. She continues, her sadness and confusion rising, until she asks how again, in the hour of her supreme distress, God can repay her so pitilessly. The voice rises, organically, to a high B-flat (at 2:35), and the notes that follow, with the tiniest of sobs at the end of the second, are almost unbearably sad, the plaint of a woman confused and in psychic pain. Callas is in perfect voice throughout, and one realizes why Puccini never cut out the aria, action-stopping or not. It defines this character's piety and passion when sung this sincerely and this movingly.

TRACK 6: PUCCINI
UN BEL DÌ VEDREMO (MADAMA BUTTERFLY)

BUTTERFLY
Un bel dì vedremo
levarsi un fil di fumo
sull'estremo confi del mare.

BUTTERFLY
One fine day we'll see
a wisp of smoke arising
over the extreme vege of the sea's horizon,

E poi la nave appare —	and afterwards the ship will appear.
poi la nave bianca	Then the white ship
entra nel porto, romba	will enter the harbor, will thunder
il suo saluto. Vedi?	a salute. You see?
È venuto!	He's arrived!
Io non gli scendo incontro.	I shan't go down to meet him.
Io no. Mi metto là	No, I shall stand there
sul ciglio del colle e aspetto,	on the brow of the hill and wait,
e aspetto gran tempo	and wait a long time,
e non mi pesa	and I shan't find
la lunga attesa.	the long wait wearisome.
E uscito dalla folla cittadina	And from the midst of the city crowd
un uom, un picciol punto	a man — a tiny speck —
s'avvia per la collina.	will make his way up the hill.
Chi sarà? chi sarà?	Who can it be?
E come sarà giunto —	And when he arrives —
Che dirà? che dirà?	what, what will he say?
Chiamerà "Butterfly!"	He'll call "Butterfly!"
dalla lontana.	from the distance.
Io senza dar risposta	Not answering, I'll
me ne starò nascosta,	remain hidden,
un po' per celia	partly to tease,
e un po' per non morir	and partly so as not to die
al primo incontro,	at the first meeting.
ed egli alquanto in pena	And, a trifle worried,
chiamerà, chiamerà:	he'll call, he'll call,
"Piccina mogliettina,	"My dear little wife,
olezzo di verbena!"	fragrance of verbena!" —
i nomi che mi dava	the names he used to call me
al suo venire.	when he came here.
Tutto questo avverrà	All this will happen,
te lo prometto.	I promise you.
Tienti la tua paura,	Keep your fears;
io con sicura fede l'aspetto.	with unalterable faith I shall wait for him.

Performing the role of Cio-Cio San in Madama Butterfly, *with tenor Giuseppe di Stefano, Chicago, 1955.*

The premiere at La Scala in 1904 of Puccini's *Madama Butterfly*—despite its featuring a cast of superb singers who were house favorites—was one of the great fiascos in the history of opera. Composer Alberto Franchetti, out for revenge for Puccini's having tricked him out of *Tosca* (see Track 5) filled the audience with hecklers who booed, laughed and otherwise fractured the event at every opportunity. In any case, the opera as performed that night was too long, the Oriental melodies and touches Puccini introduced into the score sounded merely foreign (rather than enticingly exotic); the tale of a fifteen-year-old geisha having the child of an American sailor and then committing suicide was scandalous; and the tenor role was short and included no solo. Puccini returned La Scala's money and took his opera back. After thorough revision, it was presented just three months later in Brescia and was a great success. It has remained one of opera's top-drawing works, and like *Tosca*, it has a heroine any great soprano with the right type of voice is grateful to sing.

The plot is direct: The American sailor B. F. Pinkerton "buys" the fifteen-year-old Cio-Cio-San (aka Butterfly) from a marriage broker, fully acknowledging that he does not take the union seriously. After the wedding ceremony—during which she is denounced by her relatives—and blissful wedding night, he leaves. The second act takes place three years later. Butterfly has borne Pinkerton a son and has been waiting for his return. This aria, one of the most famous in opera, comes as a response to Butterfly's maid's anxious skepticism as to whether Pinkerton will return at all. (He does, in fact, return—with an American wife—asking for the child. Butterfly requests a few moments alone and commits ritual suicide rather than live with her shame.)

Butterfly is opera's saddest, most put-upon and most innocent character. Her lack of sophistication, her forthrightness and her false optimism are heartbreaking. Callas performed the role onstage three times, all in Chicago in 1955 (she had been invited to sing it at the Met years before, but thought she was too fat at the time to be believable). This version was recorded for a recital album in 1954.

Whereas Callas used a *self-consciously* girlish voice for Lauretta in *Gianni Schicchi* (Track 3), here there's no artifice. Butterfly is only eighteen, but her past as a geisha, and the fact that she is alone in the world except for her maid and child, have matured her. She has been waiting for three years for her American "husband" to return. Although "*Un bel dì*" is clearly the opera's "hit" aria, Callas approaches it as an intimate narrative entreaty to her maid, Suzuki, to tell her what she believes, or wishes to believe,

will happen soon; events that will change their lives and bring happiness to their little household. As the aria progresses, Butterfly's vision of hope takes on more and more reality for her. For three years she has refused to despair, and she isn't going to start now.

The aria carries forward three viewpoints,: the narrator's, Butterfly's, and Pinkerton's (or what Butterfly imagines Pinkerton's will be). It starts quietly and simply, with Butterfly telling a story. At 0:37, with an image of the ship itself in her mind's eye, Butterfly-as-narrator becomes more animated; at 1:10, when she's herself again, she draws the voice and persona back modestly. She describes what her behavior will be like and the image Pinkerton making his way up the hill. "*Chi sarà? Chi sarà?*" – "Who can it be?" (2:10) continues in this little-girlish mode, quietly concentrated the way kids can be, paying close attention. When she imagines him calling her, her voice is lower and more dignified (2:24). Butterfly (as herself) continues, experiencing real anxiety when she describes how she'll remain hidden "so as not to die" (2:50 ff) at their first meeting. Her imagination runs on, evoking what he used to call her, and will again, until she snaps back to the original point of the narrative: to assure Suzuki that all will be well. And from that point on (3:30) it's all resolve, "All this will happen," sung in a more mature tone, right up until the potent, forthright high B-flat on the final words," I shall wait for him." The listener can do nothing more than hope she's right.

Playing Gilda in Verdi's Rigoletto *in Mexico City, June 1952.*

"I do not like modern music because it's all complicated. Anything that's complicated today bothers me. You see, people go to the opera to be relaxed, to have a bath of beauty... I sing the old music where, as Sir Thomas Beecham said – 'The melody is good.'"

—MARIA CALLAS,
from a televised conversation with Sir Thomas Beecham, Victor Borge and Edward R. Murrow

TRACK 7: VERDI *CARO NOME (RIGOLETTO)*

GILDA

Gualtier Maldè...nome di lui sì amato,
ti scolpisci nel core innamorato!
Caro nome che il mio cor
festi primo palpitar,
le delizie dell'amor
mi dèi sempre rammentar!
Col pensier il mio desir
a te sempre volerà,
e fin l'ultimo mio sospir,
caro nome, tuo sarà.
Col pensier, ecc.

GILDA

Walter Maldè...name of the man I love,
be thou engraved upon my lovesick heart!
Beloved name, the first to move
the pulse of love within my heart
thou shalt remind me ever
of the delights of love!
In my thoughts, my desire
will ever fly to thee,
and my last breath of life
shall be, beloved name, of thee.
In my thoughts, etc.

(Sale al terrazzo con una lanterna.)

Gualtier Maldè!
(Marullo, Ceprano, Borsa, cortigiani, armati e mascherati, vengono dalla via. Gilda entra tosto in casa.)

Caro nome, ecc.

BORSA
È là.

CEPRANO
Miratela.

CORO
Oh! quanto è bella!

MARULLO
Par fata od angiol.

CORO
L'amante è quella
di Rigoletto.

(She takes a lantern and walks up the steps to the terrace.)

Walter Maldè!
(Meanwhile, Marullo, Ceprano, Borsa and other courtiers have appeared in the road, armed and masked; they watch Gilda as she enters the house.)
Beloved name, etc.

BORSA
There she is.

CEPRANO
Look at her!

CHORUS
Oh, isn't she lovely!

MARULLO
She looks like a fairy or an angel.

CHORUS
So that's Rigoletto's mistress!

Giuseppe Verdi (1813–1901) is, arguably, Italian opera's greatest composer; indeed, in the second half of the nineteenth century in Italy, Verdi practically *was* opera. His fame in his native country was cemented early, but it was not until 1851, with *Rigoletto*, that he became internationally known as a composer. Some of that fame was extramusical: the censors found the opera's plot (taken from a play by Victor Hugo) "obscene" and "repellent," and they banned it, mainly due to the fact that it portrayed corrupt royalty. A year went by before Verdi and his librettist moved the action to that of a non-existent court in Mantua and softened some of the more pointed bits of action so that it finally could be performed.

At this point in the opera, Gilda, Rigoletto's naïve, lovely daughter, has just shared a stolen moment with the lascivious Duke, who has fooled her into believing he is a poor student named Gualtier Maldè. In this aria she reflects on that name and how dear it—and he, and their budding love—are to her. She is then abducted by the Duke's courtiers and raped by the Duke; Rigoletto swears revenge. In the last act, Rigoletto has hired an assassin to kill the Duke, but Gilda, in an act of innocent and entirely misplaced devotion to the Duke, takes his place and is, herself, murdered. She dies in Rigoletto's arms.

Callas sang Gilda early in her career, only twice in 1952, but she recorded the complete opera in 1955. The aria is a coloratura showpiece, and while Callas certainly isn't stingy with the fireworks, she has a point of view about the character and never allows the aria to turn into an empty display. Gilda is guileless, and while she is still absolutely pure, she has just tasted the possibility of real love.

She begins the recitative dreamily, repeating the name of her lover in the voice of a girl even younger and purer than Butterfly. On the word *"innamorato"* – "lovesick" (0:37), she sighs the word in a downward portamento (the gliding together of notes for a particular effect: here, just that dreaminess), which makes the word practically onomatopoetic. When the aria proper begins (1:25), she uses the rests between notes to depict a type of breathlessness and spontaneity. Each phrase is connected with more perfect examples of legato (also a smooth connecting of notes)

and, at times, upward portamento, so that the whole aria is one long thought or daydream. Her voice tapers to a mere wisp when she refers to her "last breath" (2:18 ff, with perfect trills). She continues until the word *"volera"* where, describing her thoughts "flying," the breathless, expressive staccati begin. The singing is perfect, the character remains wistful, the voice flies upward like her thoughts, culminating in a downward run and lengthy riff (beginning at 5:00 and bouncing off a high E-flat at one point): she conveys the anticipation of ecstasy. She repeats Gualtier's name, trance-like (starting at 5:55) and the aria fades away on a long-held trill—was it only a dream? (Note: The male voices heard in the background, unseen by Gilda, are her abductors.)

Maria performing Il Trovatore, *at La Scala during the 1952-53 season.*

TRACK 8: VERDI _D'AMOR SULL'ALI ROSEE (IL TROVATORE)_

LEONORA

D'amor sull'ali rosee
vanne, sospir dolente;
del prigioniero misero
conforta l'egra mente.
Com'aura di speranza
aleggia in quella stanza;
lo desta alle memorie,
ai sogni, ai sogni dell'amor.
Ma, deh! non dirgli, improvvido
le pene, le pene del mio cor! ecc.

LEONORA

On the rosy wings of love
go, oh mournful sigh;
comfort the flagging spirits
of the wretched prisoner.
Like a breath of hope
flutter in that room;
waken in him the memories,
the dreams, the dreams of love.
But, pray, don't imprudently tell him
the pangs, the pangs that rack my heart!, etc.

Il trovatore was the opera with which Verdi followed _Rigoletto_, and it's a thrill a minute. Saddled with a dreadful, confusing plot involving babies mixed up in infancy; vengeful, insane gypsy hags; and mistaken identities, Verdi nonetheless makes us care for the crude characters through his uncanny ability to portray each one's inner torments by purely musical means. Each aria—and there are plenty in this tune-filled work—telescopes a moment and a feeling, and "_D'amor sull'ali rosee_," sung by the soprano heroine Leonora at the start of the opera's last act, is a glorious example.

Leonora may be a one-dimensional character, but her love runs deep. Her lover, Manrico, is imprisoned, and here she sings, albeit in archaic terminology (she desires her "sad sigh" to fly on "rosy wings of love" to comfort him) of her love for him. All ends miserably, with Leonora taking poison after promising herself to the villainous Count di Luna, and Manrico being executed.

This aria exhibits what people mean when they speak of the "Verdi soprano." The long, arching melody requires smooth transitions up and down the scale, while the vocal line takes the voice consistently higher and higher in exposed phrases that must be sung from very quietly to very forcefully, all the while paying heed to the text and articulating carefully. An innate rhythmic sense and a command of the direction in which the music is going are crucial.

Callas sang the role 20 times, dropping it in 1955. She excelled in the role's more overtly dramatic moments, and here, if she is lacking anything at all, it is a certain sweetness of tone. Her nobility, elegance, musicality and involvement are never in doubt.

Because the images in the text are so wispy—wings of love, breath of hope, dreams of love—the aria has to be taken as a whole. In essence, it's a prayer by Leonora that her love will bring Manrico comfort while he's imprisoned. Like most of this opera, it takes place at night, and Callas's tone is hushed and covert. The first lines, with their graceful upward glides, long breath and trills, set the dark tone, and she keeps it from start to finish. Her soft attack on and fall from the high A-flat leading to and from the word "_conforta_" – "comfort" (0:43-0:50) is the equivalent of an exquisite musical sigh. Again, on the word "_memorie_" – "memory" (1:33-1:43), Callas's voice fades, just as a memory does; this is precisely the word-painting-with-notes Verdi had hoped for, and which the finest singers understand. The emphasis changes slightly when Leonora prays that Manrico won't know her pain (2:01 ff), but the mood of resignation and hope returns and carries the aria through to the end. The high notes which abound in the last third of the aria are attacked softly and, are, for the most part, quite lovely (a bit of steel occasionally creeps in where velvet would have been more welcome), though granted, it's a pity the final note is badly supported. Despite some vocal hurdles, we sense the softness and gentleness of the character.

TRACK 9: PUCCINI
IN QUELLE TRINE MORBIDE (MANON LESCAUT)

MANON

In quelle trine morbide,
nell'alcova dorata
v'è un silenzio, un gelido mortal —
v'è un silenzio,
un freddo che m'agghiaccia!
Ed io che m'ero avvezza
a una carezza voluttuosa
di labbra ardenti e d'infuocate braccia
or ho tutt'altra cosa!
O mia dimora umile,
tu mi ritorni innazi —
gaia, isolata, bianca,
come un sogno gentil e di pace e d'amor!

MANON

In those soft lace hangings,
in that gilt alcove
there is a silence, a mortal chill —
there is a silence,
a coldness that turns me to ice!
And I who was accustomed
to a voluptuous caress
of ardent lips and passionate arms
now have something quite different.
Oh, my humble dwelling,
you again appear before me —
cheerful, secluded, white-walled,
like a sweet dream of peace and love!

Giacomo Puccini, composer of
La bohème, Turandot, Tosca *and* Madama
Butterfly, *among others.*

Manon Lescaut was Puccini's first great success, the opera that put him on the map. Since Jules Massenet had already scored a great success in France with the same plot, Puccini wanted something special, and he went ruthlessly through a half-dozen librettists until he finally approved the text. Even at that, the plot deteriorates by the final act, in which we find our hero and heroine "on the plains of Louisiana," she desperate and dying, he wild with grief, exhaustion and thirst.

But until that final act, we have quite an engaging set of circumstances. Manon, in the company of her somewhat ne'er-do-well brother, stops to rest at an inn in Amiens on her way to a convent and is immediately swept off her feet by the Chevalier Des Grieux who is there with friends.

Meanwhile, the brother promises her to a wealthy, old man named Geronte, but the two of them are tricked: Des Grieux convinces Manon to run away with him, and they steal Geronte's carriage and flee to Paris. By the second act, Manon has left the penniless Des Grieux for the riches of Geronte, and she is living with him in the lap of luxury. At this moment in Act II, she reflects on her wealth and how much happier she was when she experienced true passion with Des Grieux. Des Grieux eventually finds her, they stir up their old desire, Geronte discovers them together and orders her out of his house, and when her brother returns to warn her that Geronte has called the police, she gathers up her jewelry. During the extra moments her greed costs her, she is arrested. About to be deported, Des Grieux begs to go with her. They wind up in Louisiana, where she dies.

Manon is a complicated character, at once loving and greedy, victimizer and victim. She's young, but by the time she comes to sing "*In quelle trine morbide*" she has already sadly realized what she exchanged for love: the fickle Manon here exposes her vulnerable self.

Callas never sang the role on stage, and aside from a complete portrayal of the opera in the recording studio in 1957, this aria and one from the last act, recorded in 1954, demonstrate her only thoughts on the opera.

The mood is set immediately. Manon sings as if the ideas have just dawned on her; she is experiencing a moment of self-realization. Feeling the softness around her, she nonetheless suddenly experiences a "*gelido mortal*" – "mortal chill" that "turns her to ice" (0:40-0:59). When she recalls her former passion (1:20 ff), voice and volume rise in recalled ecstasy; remembering their "humble dwelling" (1:44) she softens, but the longing rises again in her before she acknowledges that her past is now like a "sweet dream" (2:14) of peace and love. On this note, the aria ends sadly and wistfully.

TRACK 10: PUCCINI *MI CHIAMANO MIMÌ (LA BOHÈME)*

MIMÌ
Sì. Mi chiamano Mimì,
ma il mio nome è Lucia.
La storia mia è breve.
A tela o a seta
ricamo in casa e fuori.
Son tranquilla e lieta
ed è mio svago
far gigli e rose.
Mi piaccion quelle cose
che han sì dolce malia
che parlano d'amor, di primavere,
che parlano di sogni e di chimere,
quelle cose che han nome poesia…
Lei m'intende?
Mi chiamano Mimì.
Il perchè non so.
Sola, mi fo il pranzo
da me stessa.
Non vado sempre a messa,
ma prego assai il Signor.
Vivo sola, soletta,
là in una bianca cameretta;
guardo sui tetti e in cielo.
Ma quando vien lo sgelo

MIMÌ
Yes. They call me Mimì,
but my real name's Lucia.
My story is brief.
I embroider silk and satin
at home or outside.
I'm tranquil and happy,
and my pastime
is making lilies and roses.
I love all things
that have gentle magic,
that talk of love, of spring,
that talk of dreams and fancies —
the things called poetry…
Do you understand me?
They call me Mimì —
I don't know why.
I live all by myself
and I eat alone.
I don't often go to church,
but I like to pray.
I stay all alone
in my tiny white room
I look at the roofs and the sky.
But when spring comes

il primo sole è mio	the sun's first rays are mine.
il primo bacio dell'aprile è mio!	April's first kiss is mine, is mine!
il primo sole è mio.	The sun's first rays are mine!
Germoglia in un vaso una rosa,	A rose blossoms in my vase,
foglia a foglia l'aspiro.	I breathe its perfume, petal by petal.
Così gentil è il profumo d'un fior.	So sweet is the flower's perfume,
Ma i fior ch'io faccio, ahimè,	But the flowers I make, alas,
i fior ch'io faccio,	the flowers I make, alas,
ahimè non hanno odore.	alas, have no scent.
Altro di me non le saprei narrare.	What else can I say?
Sono la sua vicina	I'm your neighbor, disturbing you
che la vien fuori d'ora a importunare.	at this impossible hour.

What can one say about Puccini's *La bohème*? Along with *Aida* and *Carmen*, it is one of the world's most frequently performed and favorite operas. It presents characters who are easy to relate to in very human situations, and they sing easy-to-remember melodies which tug at our heartstrings.

Mimì is our heroine, and we meet her in the first act when she climbs the stairs to her fellow bohemians' attic to get a light for her candle. There she meets Rodolfo, who is to be the love of her life. He tells her who he is in an aria, and this is her response—it perfectly introduces us to this frail, open and honest woman.

This is another role Callas only recorded. There were plenty of fine, lyric sopranos performing Mimì in the '50s, and while what Callas brings to the role is wonderful, she obviously did not feel compelled to play it. Nevertheless, what she expresses about the character is quite moving and telling.

Although there are fine details here, as in the *Trovatore* aria (Track 8), it's really the overall feel that matters. Mimì is not a forceful personality, she's weak and what she does for a living—embroidering flowers—is simple. She's shy as well, only opening up when she speaks of spring and its sunshine and flowers. Her slide up to a soft high A on the word "*primavere*" "spring" (1:07 ff) is ravishing, as are the other truly soft touches throughout the narrative. Reiterating her name (1:52), she seems a bit more comfortable with Rodolfo, and when she sings of what spring brings (2:36 ff), the voice gathers strength and enthusiasm, which, in context, is thrilling because it seems so genuine. Then, comparing her false flowers to those of spring (4:02), her humility couldn't be lovelier, and this feeling prevails to the aria's end. What beautiful singing; what a lovely character!

TRACK 11: PUCCINI
DONDE LIETA USCI (MIMÌ'S FAREWELL) (LA BOHÈME)

MIMÌ	MIMÌ
Donde lieta uscì al tuo grido	Back to the place I left
d'amore torna sola Mimì.	at the call of your love,
Al solitario nido	I'm going back alone
ritorna un'altra volta	to my lonely nest
a intesser finti fior.	to make false flowers.
Addio senza rancor.	Goodbye…no hard feelings.
Ascolta, ascolta.	But listen.
Le poche robe aduna che lasciai	Please gather up the few things
sparse. Nel mio cassetto	I've left behind. In the trunk
stan chiusi quel cerchietto	there's the little bracelet
d'or e il libro di preghiere.	and my prayer book. Wrap them
Involgi tutto quanto in un grembiale	in an apron and I'll send
e manderò il portiere…	someone for them…
Bada, sotto il guanciale	Wait! Under the pillow
c'è la cuffietta rosa.	there's my pink bonnet.
Se vuoi…serbarla a ricordo d'amor…	If you want…keep it in memory of our love.
Addio, senza rancor.	Goodbye, no hard feelings.

By the opera's third act, Mimì and Rodolfo have broken up. Not only is he jealous of every move she makes, he can't bear to watch her suffer in their poor circumstances. Mimì is already quite ill in this scene, where she comes to say goodbye to Rodolfo with no hard feelings ("*senza rancor*").

The enchanting, modest girl we met in the previous aria is still present. But she's grown, and her sadness here is clear. Mimì sings with her usual timidity. She's trying not to break down in tears but when she pictures herself alone (0:26 ff), it almost undoes her, and here Callas adds a bit of a catch to the voice. The first times she sings "*addio senza rancor*" (0:52–1:03) it's uninflected, but she isn't ready to go: "Listen," she interrupts herself, and reminds Rodolfo to wrap a few of her possessions. Almost done again, she drags the scene out a bit longer, reminding Rodolfo of the bonnet she kept under her pillow

("*Bada…*"; 2:02 ff), telling him that he can keep it if he wishes, as a reminder of their love. Here, her voice, like their love, soars. Then, finally "*Addio, addio senza rancor,*" with a deeper emphasis on the second "*addio*" and a voice that finally trails away with an unmatchable sadness. Throughout, the singing is perfect: Callas obeys all of Puccini's instructions regarding tempo, volume, length of held notes, shadings, etc. Although we don't think of her as a shrinking violet, it's amazing what comes from Callas's respect for the music and her voice with "a thousand colors."

Maria speaking to reporters at a press conference in Paris, 1958. Despite the negative press that Maria began to receive in 1959, the Parisians continued to adore and support her.

TRACK 12: CILEA
IO SON L'UMILE ANCELLA (ADRIANA LECOUVREUR)

ADRIANA

Ecco: respiro appena.

Io son l'umile ancella

del Genio creator:

ei m'offre la favella,

il la diffondo ai cuor.

Del verso io son l'accento,

l'eco del dramma umano,

il fragile strumento

vassallo della man.

Mite, gioconda, atroce,

mi chiamo Fedeltà;

un soffio è la mia voce,

che al nuovo dì morrà.

ADRIANA

See: I am barely breathing.

I am the humble servant

of the creative Genius:

he gives me the word,

I pass it on to people's hearts.

I am only the accent of his verse,

the echo of the human drama,

the fragile instrument

he plays on with his hand.

Mild, joyous, atrocious,

I am called Faithfulness:

my voice is a breath

which will die on the morrow.

Verismo composer Francesco Cilea (1866–1950) is known almost exclusively for his 1902 opera, *Adriana Lecouvreur*. His music is filled with dramatic outbursts, enjoyable tunes and unabashed sentiment, and while individual moments touch the heart, the piece rarely probes deeply into the souls or psyches of its characters. The character of Adriana Lecouvreur is based on the life of an eponymous eighteenth-century French actress, and this is her opening aria. She has been rehearsing a speech from one of her roles, and here, she claims that she is merely the "handmaiden of her art." She meets her demise when her rival for the love of Maurizio,

the Count of Saxony, sends her violets laced with poison. She sniffs, she dies.

Callas never sang the role on stage, and after recording Adriana's two arias in 1954, she seems to have lost any interest she might have had in the character.

There's nothing special here, the performance is merely an exercise in mood, albeit a pretty one. Her opening tone is one of modesty and she sustains it throughout; when she claims that it is her job to pass the words of a play into people's hearts (1:10 ff), she draws the phrase inward. She actually accentuates the word "*accento*" (1:34) effectively, and sounds awe-struck by her own insignificance in comparison to "his [the playwright's] hand;" to emphasize this, she dips into a type of reverential chest-voice (1:57 ff). She continues to describe herself: her voice is "a breath which will die on the morrow" (2:45 to the end), softer and softer until she disappears, fading into the ether.

TRACK 13: VERDI *AH! FORS'È LUI (LA TRAVIATA)*

VIOLETTA

Ah, fors è lui che l'anima
solinga ne' tumulti
godea sovente pingere
de' suoi colori occulti!
Lui che modesto e vigile
all'egre soglie ascense,
e nuova febbre accese,
destandomi all'amor.
A quell'amor ch'è palpito
dell' universo intero,
misterioso, altero,
croce e delizia al cor!

VIOLETTA

Ah, perhaps he is the one
whom my soul,
lonely in the tumult, loved
to imagine in secrecy!
Watchful though I never knew it,
he came here while I lay sick,
awakening a new fever,
the fever of love,
of love which is the very breath
of the universe itself —
Mysterious and noble,
both cross and ecstasy of the heart

Verdi was never one to run from controversy, and *La traviata* was his foray into subject matter which was certain to upset the conservative censors. Focusing on the life of a consumptive courtesan with a good heart, and on the middle-class young man she is seen to be corrupting, Verdi had to move the action from the present back to 1700 in order to get the work performed. It was a failure at its opening; the presumably weak, frail character of Violetta was sung by a big and fat soprano, the tenor (Alfredo, her lover) was hoarse and the baritone (Germont) yelled mercilessly. By the last act, the audience was laughing out loud.

"Time will tell," Verdi said of the opera's initial failure, and he has been vindicated. *La traviata* is beautiful and memorable, dramatic tension is ever-present, and the characters are well-drawn—particularly that of Violetta. First, she renounces the wealthy courtesan's life for the true love of Alfredo but then she renounces Alfredo, whom she has been supporting, at the

The grief-stricken Violetta in La traviata, La Scala, *1955.*

request of his father, Germont, so that his family can keep its bourgeois respectability. After being publicly humiliated by Alfredo at the close of the second act, she dies of consumption in the third, with grief-stricken Alfredo, who has finally learned the truth, and Germont by her side.

Violetta played a major part in Callas's career. She sang 63 performances of the work, beginning in Florence in 1951 and ending in Dallas in 1958. Violetta is only one of the strong (or seemingly-strong) women in Callas's repertoire who wind up victimized and martyred: Anna Bolena, Tosca and Norma are three others, and together they make up about 200 of her on-stage performances. Her portrayal of them is so uncanny that one can't help but assume that she personally identified with these put-upon women.

This and the following selection come from a live performance in Lisbon in 1958. They are fascinating examples of Callas not necessarily in prime voice but remarkably affecting. Both show us Violetta's private side;

the first as she contemplates the possibility of love, the second as she is dying.

In the first act, the guests at Violetta's party have left and she is alone with her thoughts. A young man, Alfredo, has confessed that he has loved her for a year, and though she is seemingly happy with her carefree, glamorous life as a courtesan, she reflects on the situation. "*Ah, fors'è lui*" – "Ah, perhaps he is the one," she begins, as if thinking out loud. Callas emphasizes the word "*lui*" – "him" and lingers over it. The tone is tender, the two high As are whispered, as if the suggestion is coming from her subconscious. From 1:00, when she reflects on how he has watched her, her ardor rises, peaking on the word "*amor*" –"love" (1:25), which she then allows herself to analyze: the concept, which she has so long ignored, is sinking in. The coloratura flourishes that follow (2:40) are not just to show off; her thoughts are taking wing, leading to the realization that love truly is "the cross and ecstasy of the heart." She ends the aria quietly, still introspective, seemingly at peace with the idea.

TRACK 14: VERDI
ADDIO, DEL PASSATO (LA TRAVIATA)

VIOLETTA

Addio, del passato bei sogni ridenti,
le rose del volto già sono pallenti;
l'amore d'Alfredo perfino mi manca,
conforto, sostegno dell'anima stanca —
conforto, sostegno —

VIOLETTA

Goodbye, sweet, happy dreams of the past,
the roses of my cheeks are already fading.
I miss so much Alfredo's love,
which once solaced my weary soul —
Solaced and comforted —

Ah, della traviata sorridi all desio;   Ah, smile upon the woman who has strayed;
a lei, deh, perdona; tu accoglila, o Dio!   forgive her, Oh God, grant she may come to
     thee!

Ah! — Tutto, tutto finì, or tutto, tutto finì.   Now all is finished, all is over.

Here, in the opera's last act, Violetta is near death and she knows it. She sings a farewell to the happy dreams of her past and prays for God's forgiveness.

The sickly, white tone, devoid of energy with which she has begun, is sustained more-or-less throughout. Only occasionally does this Violetta gather strength to sing out. Once (0:50) is when she recalls Alfredo's love and how it consoled her. At another (1:10), she sounds half-dead but sadly comforted. Only when her thoughts again turn to God (1:53), a bit of fire burns in this pathetic creature; her tone remains firm for a few seconds but the dying character can't sustain it. The almost-inaudible tone that she then pushes to its limit (2:31) is heart-rending, and from then on (2:48 ff), as she sings "all is over, all is finished," we know she's right. The final high A, which is supposed to be a sliver of sound, is even weaker than necessary here: Callas was not in particularly secure voice and the note just about escapes her.

In an interview in *Life* magazine, Callas said about Violetta, "I see the role, and therefore the voice, as fragile, weak and delicate. It is a trapeze part filled with sick pianissimo." That is precisely what is conveyed here.

Violetta bids Germont (baritone Ettore Bastianini) farewell. La Scala, 1955.

Maria as Anna Bolena at La Scala, 1957. Maria personally oversaw the design and construction of all of her elaborate gowns.

TRACK 15: DONIZETTI
AL DOLCE GUIDAMI CASTEL NATIO (ANNA BOLENA)

ANNA

Al dolce guidami castel natio,
ai verdi platani, al queto rio
che I nostri mormora sospiri ancora.
Ah! colà, dimentico de scorsi affanni,
un giorno rendimi de' miei prim'anni,
un giorno [solo] rendimi del nostro amor.

ANNA

Lead me to the dear castle where I was born,
to the green plane trees, to that brook
that still murmurs to our sighs…
Ah! there I forget past griefs
give me back one day of my youth,
give me back one [single] day of our love.

As mentioned earlier, Gaetano Donizetti (1797–1848) was one of the trio of composers who wrote works of "bel canto." He composed more than 70 operas, many to terrible librettos, many of so-so quality, but also some in which his creative flame burned brilliantly. His best operas have a forward propulsion that is dramatic in itself, as well as handsome tunes in arias, duets and larger ensembles, vehicles for vocal display which are bound to please and excite, plot lines which are direct, and characters, who, while not psychologically deep, provide *moments* of great depth and feeling, beautifully captured and conveyed.

Anna Bolena premiered in 1830, and brought him his first international success, despite more than thirty operas of his having been performed in Italy already. It is a remarkable, rich work, concerning Henry VIII's tiring of Ann Boleyn and falling under the spell of Jane Seymour; all three characters are well-drawn and have mar-velous music. But it is Anna who carries the day—her role was composed for Giuditta Pasta, who also created Norma and Amina, the soprano lead in *La sonnambula*. (Pasta was considered the greatest singing actress of her time, and contemporary reviews read eerily like reviews of Callas's performances.)

The opera enjoyed great success for a half century before practically disappearing from the repertory. But in 1957, at La Scala, it was revived after 80 years' absence for Callas, the success was overwhelming, and it has regained its place among Donizetti's greatest operas. Callas sang it a total of twelve times during the 1957 and 1958 seasons. It was one of her greatest triumphs, with nothing lacking. On opening night, half the audience was standing and cheering before the music ended.

This aria comes near the opera's close. Anna, perhaps the ultimate wronged and abused heroine, is nearly mad as she awaits execution in her cell. In a moment of repose, she touchingly asks to be taken back to the place she was born and recalls her young love for Riccardo Percy. It is an exquisite sad aria filled with wistfulness and melancholy, and it was taped at a live performance at La Scala.

Anna is exhausted and has given up, and she sings as if in a trance. It is a mood piece which, in pure bel canto tradition, relies on certain purely vocal skills to make its emotional point. When Anna speaks of a murmuring brook ("*rio*") in her memory and how it reflected her sighs ("*sospiri*"), there are expressive trills in both phrases (0:28–0:35; 0:44–0:57). Note particularly the long melisma on the word "*ancora*" –

"still" or "yet," as if the experience is still going on. The elegantly melodic vocal line continues and Callas colors each word, using a smooth legato to turn the memory into an immediate event. The ravishing ascending spiral of notes on "*del nostro amor*" – "of our love" disappears (2:09 ff), and so does the experience: it has been imagined. The beautiful cadenza near the end, up to a B-flat (3:07), eventually lands on a soft, middle F, with the note and phrase fading away on the word "love," just as, in Anna's life, love has faded away. The long phrases, trills, and twisting vocal line are never just for show; they reflect Anna's condition. Ravishing.

TRACK 16: VERDI
UNA MACCHIA È QUI TUTTORA! (MACBETH)

LADY MACBETH

Una macchia è qui tuttora…
Via, Ei dico, o maledetta!
Una…due…gli è questa l'ora!
Tremi tu?…non osi entrar?
Un guerrier così codardo?
Oh, vergogna!…orsù, t'affretta!
Chi poteva in quel vegliardo
lanto sangue immaginar?
Chì poveta…immaginar?
Di Fiffe il Sire
sposo e padre or or non era?
Che ne avvenne?
E mai pulire queste mani io non saprò?

LADY MACBETH

Here's a spot still…
Out, I say, damned spot!
One…two…this is the time!
You tremble? Do you not dare go in?
A soldier and so afeared?
O fie!…Come, make haste!
Who would have thought that
the old man had so much blood in him?
Who could have imagined it?
The Thane of Fife
was he but now not husband and father?
What became of him?
And will these hands ne'er be clean?

No, mai pulire io non saprò!	No, I can ne'er make them clean again!
Di sangue umano	Here's the smell
sa qui sempre…Arabia intera	of human blood still…All
Rimondar sì picco! mano	the perfumes of Arabia
co' suoi balsami non può,	cannot cleanse this little hand,
…no, no, non può…	…no, they cannot…
Ohimè!	…Alas!
I panni indossa	Put on your
della notte…Or via, ti sbratta!	nightgown…Come, wash your hands!
Banco è spento, e dalla fossa	Banquo's dead and the dead
chi morì non surse ancor.	have never risen from the grave.
A letto a letto…	To bed, to bed…
Sfar non puoi la cosa fatta…	What's done cannot be undone…
Batte alcuno!	Someone's knocking. Come, Macbeth,
Andiam, Macbetto!	let not your pallor betray you.
Andiam, Macbetto, no,	Someone's knocking!
non t'accusi	Come, Macbeth!
il tuo pallor, ecc.	Come, Macbeth, no,
	let not your pallor betray you, etc.

Macbeth was Verdi's first attempt at setting a Shakespeare play to music and is rightly considered the finest of his early operas. It premiered in 1847 and revised in 1865; it is the later version that is performed nowadays. It contains the occasional weakness and awkwardness, but its dark, grave atmosphere is enormously effective. It follows the play closely and economically, and Lady Macbeth emerges as a character just as important as Macbeth. Both are well wrought, both have superb music to distinguish them, and Verdi made it clear that acting was to be as important as singing.

"Lady Macbeth's voice must be hard, stifled and dark," Verdi wrote, and indeed, the role is a notorious voice-wrecker. It requires stamina, two-octave leaps, trills, a dark chest register, strong, bright high notes, coloratura ability and an ability to exclaim almost violently—these last two being almost mutually exclusive in a soprano voice. Most sopranos steer clear of it.

Callas sang five performances of it at La Scala in 1952, and she epitomized the heartless, ruthless, malevolent, character so convincingly that many later argued that Lady Macbeth's anger and cruel ambition were not

Maria in her first of five performances of Verdi's Macbeth, *in December, 1952 at La Scala. She effectively fulfilled Verdi's wish that the voice be "harsh, choked, dark....a veiled, black voice."*

unlike the diva's. This recording was made in a studio in 1958.

It is the famous Sleepwalking Scene, wherein the guilty and unhinged lady attempts to wipe blood from her hands, recalling the murders and her disgust at her cowardly husband.

A masterpiece of mood and expression, the scene begins before the Lady's entrance. It is late at night, and the orchestra—muted strings, solo clarinet and English horn (no high winds or bright brass here)—set the scene; the trills on the winds are unsettling. The music suggests wandering and restlessness and it is marked to be played very quietly, coming out of its slumber only once, briefly (1:15ff), only to return again to pianississimo immediately. Strings and winds alternate until 1:30, when the strings carry a melody and the winds rock back and forth sleepily underneath.

Her first words, sung as in a trance, are clearly those of a deranged mind (3:37); she sees the nonexistent blood on her hand and begins to obsess on the "damned spot" (3:55), which of course, represents the evil deeds she cannot erase. She addresses an imaginary Macbeth: "_Tremi tu?…non osi entrar?_" – "Are you trembling? Do you dare not go in?" (4:13–4:26). This is sung with a type of scorn a composer cannot write— he can only hope the singer will be able to express it. She recalls the copious amount of blood that flowed from King Duncan after the murder—who could have imagined so much? The final "_immaginar_" (5:22–5:31) is so filled with disbelief and horror that she (vocally) shrinks

from it. "_Che n'avvenne?_ – "What became of him?" (5:55) is a disjointed thought, as if she's been awakened from her reverie, but she's soon preoccupied with her bloody hands again, realizing with both horror and resignation that they'll never be clean, even with all of Arabia's perfumes (6:50–7:45).

She sighs ("_Ohimè!_"), exhausted, and tells the still-absent Macbeth to put on his night clothes, recalling that Banquo is dead and assuring him (and herself?) that the dead can't rise again (8:10ff). She calls Macbeth to bed ("_a letto_") almost matter-of-factly because "what's done is done," but the hallucinations begin again and she imagines someone knocking (9:00 and 9:24) as they did after the murder, and fears that they will see how pale and guilty Macbeth is. She calls to him repeatedly, her voice rising nervously above the staff (up to this point she has remained in the lower and middle thirds of her voice), as she begins to leave the scene to continue her wandering. And as she recedes into the darkness of the castle, the voice flies to an unearthly region a bit more than two octaves above her lowest note—a high D-flat (10:22ff). Verdi marked the note to be sung with a "_fil de voce_" (a wisp of a voice), and the effect, as you can hear, is bone-chilling.

By turns hollow-voiced, fierce, malevolent, vulnerable, disdainful and occasionally limpid, Callas truly seems haunted; the scene is as much acted as sung. Is it possible to separate the singer from the song in a performance as complete as this?

Compact Disc 2

TRACK 1: GLUCK
J'AI PERDU MON EURYDICE (ORPHÉE ET EURYDICE)

ORPHEE	ORPHEUS
J'ai perdu mon Eurydice,	I have lost my Eurydice,
rien n'égale mon malheur;	nothing equals my unhappiness.
sort cruel! quelle rigueur!	Cruel fate! what severity!
Rien n'égale mon malheur.	Nothing equals myunhappiness.
Je succombe à ma douleur.	I succumb to my grief.
Eurydice, Eurydice,	Eurydice, Eurydice,
réponds. Quel supplice!	answer. What torment!
Réponds-moi.	Answer me.
C'est ton epoux, ton epoux fidèle;	'Tis thy husband, thy faithful husband:
entends ma voix qui t'appelle.	hear my voice that calls thee.
J'ai perdu mon Euridice, etc.	I have lost my Eurydice, etc.
Mortel silence!	Mortal silence!
Vaine espérance!	Vain hope!
Quelle souffrance!	What suffering!
Quel tourment déchire mon coeur!	What torment tears my heart!
J'ai perdu mon Eurydice, etc.	I have lost my Eurydice, etc.

Christoph Willibald Gluck (1714–87) is one of the most important figures in opera. To his ears, opera had become an empty display of singers' abilities and egos; he demanded a return to clarity and simplicity. Opera was to have the directness of Greek tragedy. His later works have their basis in Greek mythology, and *Orphée et Eurydice*, his French revision of the earlier *Orfeo ed Euridice*, is a perfect example.

The musician Orphée mourns the death of his wife, Eurydice, and the God of Love tells him that he will be allowed to go to the Underworld to try to retrieve her. If he succeeds in charming the Furies (which he does), he can lead Eurydice up to the Living World...provided he does not turn around to look at her until they are out of Hades. He looks back—and she is taken from him. This aria, an exquisite,

The French Arias, recorded in 1961.

top of her range, while exploiting the rich middle and bottom of her voice.

This is a stunning rendition, solemn and filled with unbounded sadness. The opening lines are sung with little emphasis; the dusky tone of lamentation says it all. On the word *"douleur"* – "grief" (0:54) the tone darkens just a bit more, and the heaviness persists until a truly heartbreaking *"Réponds-moi"* – "Answer me" (leading up to 1:23). A total change occurs when Orphée sadly, but with a light lovingness, identifies himself as the faithful husband. There's true, hopeless desperation in the second calls of *"Eurydice, Eurydice"* (2:26 ff), so much more dire than the first.

But one has only to listen to the three times Orphée repeats his opening lines—*"J'ai perdu mon Eurydice"* (the opening, 1:48 and 3:10)—to realize what altered coloring of the same notes can do for dramatic underpinning. And that was one of Callas's great gifts.

simple outpouring of grief, is his lament at having lost her again. (Love soon takes pity on him and returns her; all ends happily in the opera, if not in the myth.)

Callas never sang this role on stage, and this aria, recorded in 1961, marked her increasing interest in the French repertoire (with which, it turned out, at least on recordings, she had a great affinity), as well as in music composed for a voice pitched lower than the roles she had based her career on. This allowed her to avoid the ever-more troublesome, at times dreadful,

TRACK 2:
L'AMOUR EST UN OISEAU REBELLE (*CARMEN*)

CARMEN
L'amour est un oiseau rebelle,
que nul ne peut apprivoiser,
et c'est bien en vain qu'on l'appelle,
s'il lui convient de refuser.
Rien n'y fait, menace ou prière,
l'un parle bien, l'autre se tait;
et c'est l'autre que je préfère,

CARMEN
Love is a rebellious bird,
whom none can tame;
vainly one calls him
if it suits him to refuse.
Nothing serves, neither threat nor prayer,
one speaks fair, the other is dumb;
and 'tis the latter that I prefer,

il n'a rien dit; mais il me plaît.
L'amour est enfant de Bohème,
il n'a jamais, jamais connu de loi,
si tu ne m'aimes pas, je t'aime;
et si je t'aime, prends garde à toi!

L'oiseau que tu croyais surprendre
battit de l'aile et s'envola;
l'amour est loin, tu peux l'attendre;
tu ne l'attends plus, il est là!
Tout autour de toi, vite, vite,
il vient, s'en va, puis il revient;
tu crois le tenir, il t'évite;
tu crois l'éviter, il te tient!
L'amour est enfant de Bohème, etc.

he has said nothing; but he pleases me.
Love is a gypsy child,
he has never, never known law,
if you do not love me, I love you;
and if I love you, beware!

The bird that you thought to surprise
beat his wing and flew away;
love is far, you may await him;
when you wait no longer, he is there!
All around you, quickly, quickly
he comes, goes, then he returns;
you think to catch him, he avoids you;
you think to escape him, he sticks close to you.
Love is a gypsy child, etc.

Georges Bizet (1838–75) needs little introduction, even to those who know little about opera. As the composer of *Carmen*, he is part of our collective unconscious—the heroine's Habanera and Seguidilla and the bullfighter's Toreador Song are instantly recognizable melodies. The tale of the thoroughly independent, outwardly sexual gypsy temptress who leads a young soldier to ruin—and eventually to kill her—has fascinated since the opera's premiere over 125 years ago.

With the sarcasm, self-sufficiency, sex-appeal and anger inherent in the character, Callas would have been superb as Carmen onstage, but never performed it. She did, however, record the entire opera in 1964, and it is a classic: this and the next aria are taken from that recording.

In this aria, Carmen's entrance, she flirts with the men outside the cigarette factory at which she works. She compares love to a wild bird and a gypsy-child—untamable and unpredictable—and warns that any man Carmen chooses to love should beware.

What can one possibly do with a "hit" such as the Habanera? It is so familiar that we think anyone can sing it. This may be true, but Callas, through some odd phrasings and linking of notes, makes it unique.

Callas's Carmen is almost aristocratic, but she's an aristocrat who saunters. She begins quietly and only alters the volume near then end of each verse, to let the men know that she's through. She skips a pause between lines (0:18 to 0:24), allowing for no argument from anyone, with a fascinating register-changing slide through notes. After the repeated "*L'amour*"s, each with a different emphasis, she eases into the melody again; the warning "If I love you, be careful" (1:18–1:32) leaves no room for misinterpretation, and with the same words she ends the first verse even more ferociously (1:55–2:05): any man who tries is going to get what he deserves. In the second verse, too, certain words are underlined: "*jamais*" – "never," and, of course, "*l'amour,*" which is never sung the same way twice. (At 3:30) the "*Prends garde à toi!*" – "Be careful!" manages to be both alluring and treacherous— and isn't that exactly what Carmen is?

TRACK 3: BIZET
PRÈS DE REMPARTS DE SÉVILLE (SEGUIDILLA) (CARMEN)

CARMEN
Près des remparts de Séville,
chez mon ami Lillas Pastia,
j'irai danser la séguedille,
et boire du manzanilla.
J'irai chez mon ami Lillas Pastia!
Oui, mais toute seule on s'ennuie,
et les vrais plaisirs sont à deux.
Donc, pour me tenir compagnie,
j'emmènerai mon amoureux!
Mon amoureux…il est au diable:
je l'ai mis à la porte hier.
Mon pauvre coeur très consolable,
mon coeur est libre comme l'air.
J'ai des galants à la douzaine,
mais ils ne sont pas à mon gré.
Voice la fin de la semaine,
qui veut m'aimer? je l'aimerai
Qui veut mon âme? Elle est à prendre!
Voux arrivez au bon moment!
Je n'ai guère le temps d'attendre,
car avec mon nouvel amant…

CARMEN
By the ramparts of Seville,
at my friend Lillas Pastia's place,
I'm going to dance the seguidilla
and drink manzanilla.
I'm going to my friend Lillas Pastia's!
Yes, but all alone one gets bored,
and real pleasures are for two.
So, to keep me company,
I shall take my lover!
My lover…he's gone to the devil:
I showed him the door yesterday.
My poor heart, so consolable —
my heart is as free as air.
I have suitors by the dozen,
but they are not to my liking.
Here we are at the week end;
Who wants to love me? I'll love him.
Who wants my heart? It's for the taking!
You've come at the right moment!
I have hardly time to wait,
for with my new lover…

Près des remparts de Séville, etc.

JOSÉ
Tais-toi! je t'avais dit de ne pas me parler!

CARMEN
Je ne te parle pas,
je chante pour moi-même;
et je pense…il ne'est pas défendu de penser!
Je pense à certain officier,
qui m'aime, et qu'à mon tour,
oui, à mon tour je pourrais bien aimer!

JOSÉ
Carmen!

CARMEN
Mon officier n'est pas un capitaine,
pas même un lieutenant,
il n'est que brigadier;
mais c'est assez pour une bohémienne,
et je daigne m'en contenter!

JOSÉ
(déliant la corde qui attache les mains de
    Carmen)
Carmen, je suis comme un homme ivre,
si je cède, si je me livre,
ta promesse, tu la tiendras,
ah! si je t'aime, Carmen, tu m'aimeras?

CARMEN
Oui…
Nous danserons la séguedille

By the ramparts of Seville, etc.

JOSÉ
Stop! I told you not to talk to me!

CARMEN
I'm not talking to you,
I'm singing to myself;
and I'm thinking…It's not forbidden to think!
I'm thinking about a certain officer
who loves me,
and whom in my turn I might really love!

JOSÉ
Carmen!

CARMEN
My officer's not a captain,
not even a lieutenant,
he's only a corporal;
but that's enough for a gypsy girl
and I'll deign to content myself with him!

JOSÉ
(untying Carmen's hands)

Carmen, I'm like a drunken man,
if I yield, I'll give in,
you'll keep your promise?
Ah! if I love you. Carmen, you'll love me?

CARMEN
Yes…
We'll dance the seguidilla

en buvant du manzanilla.

JOSÉ
Chez Lillas Pastia…
Tu le promets!
Carmen…
Tu le promets!

CARMEN
Ah! Près des remparts de Séville, etc.

while we drink manzanilla.

JOSÉ
At Lillas Pastia's…
You promise!
Carmen…
You promise!

CARMEN
Ah! By the ramparts of Seville, etc.

One man who has paid Carmen no any attention at all is the soldier, Don José. After she is arrested for fighting and put in his care, she seduces him with this aria, inviting him to a rendezvous at the tavern of her friend, Lillas Pastia, where she will dance a gypsy dance, the Seguidilla, for him, and more.

Although, like the Habanera, this can be a showpiece, Callas sings it more intimately, to Don José alone. The first lines are a straight invitation, with no emphasis. When she refers to her dismissed lover (0:57), her tiny laugh is derisive; if Don José were smart, which he's not, he'd run. Then she again makes that upward glide through notes and registers (1:27 ff). The unevenly produced tone, a liability in many singers (and a true vocal weakness at this point in Callas's career), is here turned into sex appeal. The reprise of the invitation is sung in chest voice, more emphatically (1:40). In her dialogue with the poor, already smitten Don José (starting at 2:10), her sar-

castic tone both angers and excites him, and she makes it clear to us that she is not only interested in him (3:02 ff) but, more dangerously, she knows she's got him hooked. As he turns more and more desperate (4:04; he's energetically sung here by tenor Nicolai Gedda), she reprises the original tune and words using a big, emphatic tone and ending on a whipped high B-natural that lets us know just how derisively Don José is going to be dismissed…as soon as he unties her wrists, which he foolishly does as the aria concludes.

Bizet's Carmen, *recorded in 1964.*

Maria in a performance of Rossini's Il barbiere di Siviglia *staged at* La Scala in 1956. Maria delivered an awkward and ill-received performance, more shrew than vixen.

"One especially sensed the warlike climate of the Scala audience during the Callas era. When her Rosina was whistled and hissed, people went home content. This even though Maria was the prize of the theater, greatly admired, even to the point of idolatry. As such, she became a target."

—CONDUCTOR CARLO MARIA GIULINI

TRACK 4: ROSSINI
UNA VOCE POCO FA (IL BARBIERE DI SIVIGLIA)

ROSINA

Una voce poco fa
qui nel cor mi risuonò,
il mio cor ferito è già,
e Lindor fu che il piagò.
Sì, Lindoro mio sarà,
lo giurai, la vincerò, ecc.
Il tutor ricuserà,
io l'ingegno aguzzerò,
alla fin s'accheterà,
e contenta io resterò.
Sì, Lindoro mio sarà, ecc.
Io son docile, son rispettosa,
sono obbediente, dolce, amorosa.
Mi lascio reggere, mi lascio reggere,
mi fo guidar mi fo guidar.
Ma se mi toccano dov'è il mio debole
sarò una vipera, sarò
e cento trappole prima di cedere,
farò giocar, farò giocar, ecc.

ROSINA

The voice I heard just now
has thrilled my very heart.
My heart already is pierced
and it was Lindoro who hurled the dart.
Yes, Lindoro shall be mine.
I've sworn it. I'll succeed, etc.
My guardian won't consent,
but I will sharpen my wits,
and at last he will relent
and I shall be content.
Yes, Lindoro shall be mine, etc.
I am docile, I am respectful,
I am obedient, sweet and loving.
I can be ruled,
I can be guided,
but if crossed in love
I can be a viper, yes,
and a hundred tricks I shall play,
before they have their way, etc.

Gioacchino Rossini (1792–1868) completes the trio of bel canto composers, and while Bellini may have been the most melancholy and lovely and Donizetti stands out as the most urgently melodramatic, Rossini is the most entertaining. He is the master of Italian comic opera (although, since the bel canto revival Callas helped inaugurate, a dozen or so of his serious operas have been rediscovered, and they are equally fine). Between 1810 and 1840 anyone who wrote an opera in Italy was compared to Rossini; he moved to Paris in 1824 and composed his five final operas there. He retired in 1830, at the peak of his popularity, composing only small pieces and a religious work or two, preferring to throw dinner parties and comment on the world around him.

Il barbiere di Siviglia is his most famous work. It tells of the love between the foxy, clever Rosina and Count Almaviva, disguised as "Lindoro," and of the barber, Figaro, who, along with Rosina, manipulates the situation to their advantage despite Rosina's guardian's attempts to thwart their romance and marriage.

This is Rosina's entrance aria, and in the course of its six minutes, Rossini tells us everything we need to know about her. The text is clear, the music even clearer. Callas sang the role five times on stage, all at La Scala in 1956. By all reports, it was as close to a catastrophe as she ever had; even the conductor, her great admirer Carlo Maria Giulini, was horrified. Her humor was too broad and she was more shrew than vixen. She recorded the role a year or so later, by which time she had clearly digested it, honed it and toned it down, and she sang this aria occasionally in concerts later in her career.

The role was written for a mezzo-soprano but was later co-opted and altered by high sopranos. Callas returns it to the mezzo range, but with some high embellishments. Her smokey middle voice is very appealing.

This is a subdued performance and all the more powerful for that. This Rosina begins almost ruminitively, recalling the voice she's just heard; then, some nice coloratura figures flavor the words (1:00). The repeat (1:42) moves into flights of fancy with some nice fireworks (2:15), although the somewhat wobbly, steely B-natural that ends the phrase augurs badly for high notes to come. She describes herself as "docile, respectful, obedient, sweet and loving," and claims she can be "ruled and guided" (3:00–3:35). The sounds coming from Callas couldn't be lovelier, sweeter or more perfectly filigreed. "*Ma*" – "But," Rosina says, she's different when she's crossed in love. Here we realize who this girl is; as her true self starts to emerge, so do more vocal fireworks. She reiterates her docility (4:21), but then underscores how she'll play tricks on those who try to cross her. Callas isn't menacing or threatening, she's just letting us know. Her vocal agility, staccati, and runs, all learned from her teacher Elvira de Hidalgo in the best bel canto tradition, carry her brilliantly to the aria's close.

TRACK 5: MEYERBEER
OMBRA LEGGIERA (SHADOW SONG) (DINORAH)

DINORAH
Ombra leggiera,
non te n'andar,
non t'involar,
no, no, no,

DINORAH
Fleet shadow,
do not go, do not vanish,
no, no, no,
fay or fancy,

fata o chimera,
sei lusinghiera,
non t'involar,
no, no, no,
ombra, a me cara,
corriamo a gara,
resta con me,
al mio piè
ah!
non t'involar!
Ad ogni aurora
ti vo' trovar,
ah, resta ancora,
vieni a danzar,
se resterai,
se non ten vai,
m'udrai cantar,
t'appressa a me,
rispondi a me,
canta con me!
Ah! a te!
Ah! va ben!
Ah! a te!
Ah! sì, ecc.
Ombra leggiera,
non te n'andar, ecc.

you are alluring,
do not vanish,
no, no, no
shadow, dear to me,
let us race together,
stay with me,
at my heel,
oh!
do not vanish!
At every dawn
I am to find you,
ah, stay a while,
come and dance,
if you stay,
if you do not go,
you will hear me sing,
come nearer to me,
answer me,
sing with me!
Ah, now you!
Ah, just so!
Ah, now you!
Ah, yes, etc.
Fleet shadow,
do not go, etc.

Giacomo Meyerbeer (1791–1864), whose operas dominated the stage in Paris for almost fifty years, was the most overrated composer of the nineteenth century. Filled with spectacle—a ballet of dead nuns, a scene involving ice-skating—his operas are as emotionally empty as they are lavish. This is not to say that taking in an entire Meyerbeer opera might not be fun. It's merely the equivalent of having dessert for dinner.

Dinorah was one of his last works. Its pastoral Breton setting is the background for a plot involving Hoël, a goatherd, and his betrothed,

Dinorah. When a magician tells Hoël about some buried treasure, he leaves to find it; Dinorah, thinking he has abandoned her, goes mad. Wandering the hills with her goat, she spots her shadow in the moonlight and plays with it: this is the aria's "dramatic" content.

This is a showpiece for a coloratura soprano, and was Callas's only contact with Meyerbeer. She recorded it in 1954 and sang it once or twice in concert, in Italian translation. It's pure froth.

Again, the technique (and choice) reflect de Hidalgo's influence—it is fast, high, light. As light-voiced showpieces go, this is top-of-the-line, and Callas's performance is virtuosic in the extreme. The weird echo-effects as Dinorah plays with her shadow (beginning at 1:30 and almost for a minute-and-a-half), asking it to answer her and sing with her, are achieved through a drawing back of the tone in the repeated phrases. She finds shadings even the composer didn't realize were in the music. She begins again, with more variations (3:14 ff). A fabulous race to the finish (starting at 3:48) makes one wonder: Can singing for the sake of singing be any better justified? The upward runs, the interplay with the flute (4:30 ff) are delicious. A trill that doesn't quite catch leads to a cadenza, a better trill and a big, solid high D-flat designed to bring an audience to its feet. Can this be the same voice and temperament that created the sounds from *La Wally* (CD 1, Track 2)? Can one voice have such darkness and such light? The two arias were recorded in the same week.

TRACK 6: GOUNOD
JE VEUX VIVRE DANS CE RÊVE (WALTZ SONG)
(*ROMÉO ET JULIETTE*)

JULIETTE	JULIET
Ah!	Ah!
Je veux vivre	I wish to live
dans ce rêve qui m'enivre;	in this dream which intoxicates me;
ce jour encor,	this day still,
douce flamme,	sweet flame,
je te garde dans mon âme	I keep thee in my heart
comme un trésor!	like a treasure!
Cette ivresse	This intoxication
de jeunesse	of youth
ne dure, hélas! qu'un jour!	lasts, alas! but one day!

Maria at her elegant 60 Via Buonarotti address in Milan, 1957. By this time, Maria had become a trendsetter in Italy. All of her clothes were personally designed for her, and she selected the fabric for her outfits, sometimes sketching their outlines herself.

Puis vient l'heure	Then comes the hour
où l'on pleure,	when one weeps;
le coeur cède a l'amour,	the heart yields to love
et le bonheur fuit sans retour.	and happiness flies, never to return.
Je veux vivre, etc.	I wish to live, etc.
Loin de l'hiver morose	Far from gloomy winter
laisse-moi sommeiller	let me slumber,
et respirer la rose	and breathe the rose
avant de l'effeuiller.	before scattering its petals.
Ah!	Ah!
Douce flamme,	Sweet flame,
reste dans mon âme	remain in my heart
comme un doux trésor	like a sweet treasure
longtemps encore!	a long while yet!

Charles Gounod (1818–93) was one of the nineteenth century's most popular and successful composers. He is loved for his melodies, his handsome orchestration and the appealing way he wrote for the voice. If his works are neither groundbreaking nor masterpieces, they are endlessly pleasurable and make for an engrossing evening at the opera. His most famous opera is *Faust*; second is *Roméo et Juliette*.

Here, the young Juliette is at her first ball, at the center of attention. She is engaged to Paris, but, in this aria, she revels in her youth, her freedom and her ability to enjoy life.

Another coloratura showpiece, this recording was Callas's only contact with the character, and it is difficult to tell what attracted her to it, particularly so late in her career. The years between '54 and '61, when this was recorded, were hard on Callas's voice. The tone here is hardly that of a teenager, although in softer, lower passages, she does paint a picture of a girl on the brink of happiness. It starts off badly, with an ugly trill and a nasty B-flat, but once the words begin, there's some magic (the little "grace" notes on each of the first three words are lovely), and a careful following reveal niceties: a sweet breathless attack on "*douce flamme*" – "sweet flame" (0:38); a knockout upward and downward run (1:38); convincing introspection (2:10), when Juliette turns poetic about wishing to be far from winter (i.e., the opposite of youth); and nice energy whenever there's no pressure on the voice. Some of Dinorah's lightness returns (2:36 ff), but only briefly—back above the staff and at *forte* (despite a sensational riff at 3:00), she's not comfortable, and the final high C, flapping in the wind, leaves nothing but a bad taste.

TRACK 7: SAINT-SAËNS *PRINTEMPS QUI COMMENCE*
(SAMSON ET DALILA)

DALILA	DELILAH
Printemps qui commence,	Spring which is beginning,
portant l'espérance	bringing hope
aux coeurs amoureux,	to hearts in love,
ton souffle qui passe	thy passing breath
de la terre efface	from the earth wipes away
les jours malheureux.	unhappy days.
Tout brûle en notre âme,	Everything burns in our souls,
et ta douce flamme	and thy sweet flame
vient sécher nos pleurs;	comes to dry our tears;
tu rends à la terre,	thou givest to the earth,
par un doux mystère,	by a sweet mystery,
les fruits et les fleurs.	fruits and flowers.
En vain je suis belle!	In vain am I beautiful!
Mon coeur plein d'amour,	My heart, filled with love,
pleurant l'infidèle,	weeping for the unfaithful one,
attend son retour!	awaits his return!
Vivant d'espérance,	Living on hope
mon coeur désolé	my broken heart
garde souvenance	keeps the memory
du bonheur passé.	of past happiness.
À la nuit tombante	At nightfull
j'irai, triste amante,	I shall go, a sad lover,
m'asseoir au torrent,	to sit beside the stream,
l'attendre en pleurant!	awaiting him in tears!
Chassant ma tristesse,	Banishing my sorrow,
s'il revient un jour,	if he return one day,
à lui ma tendresse	to him my tenderness,
et la douce ivresse	and the sweet intoxication
qu'un brûlant amour	which a burning love
garde à son retour!	keeps for his return!
Chassant ma tristesse, etc.	Banishing my sorrow, etc.

Camille Saint-Saëns (1835–1921), French composer and child prodigy (he started composing at three and gave a recital at five), penned twelve operas, but is remembered today for only one of them: *Samson et Dalila*. Despite the fact that his works are not known for their dramatic impact, he manages to convey Dalila's sensuality in her two arias. The character is, of course, dark, and the role is correctly composed for mezzo-soprano. The rich, seductive music requires a

Maria signing autographs for enthusiastic admirers. She would eagerly have set aside her career to start a family, had either Meneghini or Onassis been willing.

smokey, suggestive tone throughout. The role sits perfectly in Callas's rich middle and lower voice, particularly by 1961 when this was recorded, but it, too, is a role she never sang on stage.

In this aria, which closes Act I, Samson, champion of the Hebrews, has just met the Philistine temptress, Dalila. He knows that he must resist her, but after she sings of Spring and the reawakening of love, he finds it impossible.

It would be easy to overdo the vampiness here, but Callas goes for a type of restrained smoldering that is irresistible. Beginning with a tone which can only be called erotic, Dalila plays with Samson for five minutes; in Callas's reading, the aria seems like one long sigh of desire. Callas conveys this through exquisite use of portamento, a smooth, deliberate sliding from note to note (with the notes slurred-over audibly, for emphasis) which creates just the comfortable mood she wants to set for Samson. The text of the first minute-and-a-half of the aria is all about the return of Spring, which brings hopes to "hearts in love;" then, the metaphors disappear (1:41) and Dalila sings of her lover, her broken heart, her sorrow and how she keeps her love burning for him. As the temperature rises, so does the volume and urgency; however, she changes to a more tender sound (2:30) to tell Samson how, at nightfall, she'll sit weeping by a stream, waiting for his return. Even when she goes into chest voice (3:48), she remains soft and pliable. Again, the tying together of notes to form phrases creates an entire mood, and that is what this aria is about.

TRACK 8: SAINT-SAËNS
MON CŒUR S'OUVRE À TA VOIX (SAMSON ET DALILA)

DALILA

Mon coeur s'ouvre à ta voix comme s'ouvrent
les fleurs aux baisers de l'aurore!
Mais, ô mon bien-aimé, pour mieux sécher mes
pleurs,

que ta voix parle encore!
Dis-moi qu'à Dalila tu reviens pour jamais!

Redis à ma tendresse
les serments d'autrefois, ces serments que j'aimois!
Ah! réponds à ma tendresse!
Verse-moi, verse-moi l'ivresse!
Réponds à ma tendresse, etc.
Ainsi qu'on voit des blés les épis onduler
sous la brise légère,
ainsi frémit mon coeur,
pret a se consoler,
À ta voix qui m'est chère!
La flèche est mois rapide à porter le trépas,
que ne l'est ton amante à voler dans tes bras!
Ah! réponds à ma tendresse!
Verse-moi, verse-moi l'ivresse!
Réponds à ma tendresse! etc.

DELILAH

My heart opens to your voice as flowers
open
to the kisses of dawn.
But, O my beloved, the better to dry my
tears,
let your voice speak once more!
Tell me that to Delilah you are returning for
ever!

Repeat, to my tenderness,
the vows of before, those vows that I loved!
Ah! respond to my tenderness!
Fill me, fill me with ecstasy!
Respond to my tenderness, etc.
As one sees the ears of corn ripple
beneath the light breeze,
so flutters my heart,
ready to take comfort
from your voice that is dear to me!
The arrow is less swift to deal destruction
than is your beloved to fly into your arms!
Ah! respond to my tenderness!
Fill me, fill me with ecstasy!
Respond to my tenderness, etc.

By its second act, Samson and Dalila have had three (offstage) encounters, but he has remained chaste. Here, he has arrived at Dalila's tent, intending to reject her. She sings this sumptuous, intense song of love to him, begging him to respond to her. He does, as we know, and the haircut he receives leads to his ruin.

This aria is more overt than the previous one; Dalila has Samson clearly within reach and is at the height of her powers. Given the heft

Callas had at the bottom of her voice, her decision to use it lightly (as she did in the earlier piece, on Track 7) throughout this aria is all the more intelligent and canny. Saint-Saëns' torrid orchestral accompaniments—one can feel the hot, desert breeze—create a sultry atmosphere, but many mezzos overstate the hip-swinging aspects of the aria. Again, Callas is subtler. The aria's text is all yearning and sexual metaphor (flowers opening, arrows that are slower than Dalila's willingness to fly into Samson's arms, etc.), and Callas's delivery is pure velvet. Referring to the vows that she has made to him (1:16), she tapers the words "I loved" – "*j'aimais*" to a whisper before entreating him to respond to her. The effect is intoxicating. The "arrow" imagery (3:19) is stronger, but it leads back into entreaties only a dead man could resist. This is a study in seduction, in which Callas uses the smokiest parts of her voice to amazing effect. "*Verse-moi l'ivresse*" – "Fill me with ecstasy," repeated at the close of each verse, is like an urgent invitation: It's amazing that Samson doesn't cut off his own hair.

TRACK 9: MASSENET
PLEUREZ, PLEUREZ MES YEUX (LE CID)

CHIMÈNE

De cet affreux combat je sors l'âme brisée!

Mais enfin je suis libre et je pourrai du moins
soupirer sans contrainte et souffrir sans témoins.

Pleurex! pleurex, mes yeux! tombez, triste rosée
qu'un rayon de soleil ne doit jamais tarir!
S'il me reste un espoir, c'est de bientôt mourir!
Pleurez, mes yeux, toutes vos larmes!
Pleurez, mes yeux!
Mais qui donc a voulu l'eternité des pleurs?
Ô chers ensevelis, trouvez-vous tant de charmes

à léguer aux vivants d'implacables douleurs?
Hélas! je me souviens, il me disait:
"Avec ton doux sourire

CHIMÈNE

From this dreadful combat I emerge broken-
hearted!

But at last I am free and I shall at least be able
to sigh without constraint and to suffer without witnesses.

Weep, weep my eyes! Fall, sad dew
that a ray of sunshiine should never dry!
If one hope remains to me, it is to die soon!
Weep, my eyes, all your tears!
Weep, weep, my eyes!
But who has wished this eternity of tears?
O dear ones in your graves, do you find such
delight
in bequeathing to the living implacable griefs?
Alas! I remember he said to me:
"With your sweet smile

tu ne saurais jamais conduire
qu'aux chemins glorieux ou qu'aux sentiers
　　bénis!"
Ah! mon père! Hélas!
Pleurez! pleurez mes yeux, etc.

you can only ever lead on
to glorious roads or blessed paths!"

Ah, my father! Alas!
Weep, weep my eyes! etc.

Jules Massenet (1842–1912) composed music of great elegance and suavity, occasionally lapsing into a type of eroticism which some find false and cloying. His operas are filled with moments of emotional intensity, and a few of them—*Manon, Werther, Le Cid*—are close to masterpieces. At his best, as in the two arias recorded performed here and on Track 10, his sincerity and his ability to catch the essence of genuine sadness are raised to epic proportions.

Le Cid is, arguably, his most heroic score, constructed on a grand scale. Rodrigue, the title character, fights a duel with the man who killed his father, Count Gormas. Gormas's daughter, Chimène, is Rodrigue's fiancée, and after Gormas is killed in the duel, Chimène is tormented by her two allegiances—to her lover and to her father. By the end of the opera, Chimène has forgiven Rodrigue and they are united.

Again, by 1961, this was the kind of role that sat in the best part of Callas's range, and she included this aria in concerts often after this recording was made.

In the opening recitative, the lamentable situation is laid out directly, and the remainder of the aria is one long study in torment and psychic pain. The aria itself (beginning at 1:50) carries a tone of resignation and gloom, and the text and music are so overwrought that the singer must be careful not to exaggerate: Callas wisely emphasizes the second *"pleurez"* – "cry" with just the tiniest catch in the voice. Oddly, when Chimène states that her only hope is to die soon (2:30), Callas gives the character a bit of strength, with that sentiment ending on a pitch-dark descent into chest voice on *"mes"* in another of the repeated calls of *"Pleurez, mes yeux"* (2:56 ff). Massenet alters the mood when Chimène rages against those who have caused her grief (3:14–3:40), and Callas hardens her tone accordingly. A further change in emphasis occurs as Chimène's thoughts turn to her father (3:50 ff), and the excitement calls forth a rise to a tough-sounding but controlled high B-flat (4:07). With the reprise of the opening text (4:47), the emotional heat and tragedy begin to mount again, culminating in a bad high A, followed by a B-natural filled with grief and despair. Love Callas or not, that note cannot be heard as anything other than ugly. Back in the middle/bottom range for the final three words, Callas moves us again as no one else can, but it's hard to forget those few, earlier punishing moments.

189

TRACK 10: MASSENET
ADIEU, NOTRE PETITE TABLE (MANON)

MANON

Je ne suis que faiblesse—et que fragilité!
Ah! malgré moi
je sens couler mes larmes
devant ces rêves effacés;
l'avenir aura-t-il les charmes
de ces beaux jours déjà passés?
Adieu, notre petite table,
qui nous réunit si souvent!
Adieu, notre petite table,
si grande pour nous cependant!
On tient, c'est inimaginable,
si peu de place en se serrant…
Adieu, notre petite table;
un même verre était le nôtre,
chacun de nous quand il buvait
y cherchait les lèvres de l'autre…
Ah! pauvre ami, comme il m'aimait!
Adieu, notre petite table, adieu!

MANON

I am nothing but weakness and frailty!
Ah! despite myself,
I feel my tears flowing
before those vanished dreams!
Will the future have the charms
of those fair days already passed?
Goodbye, our little table,
where we so often are joined!
Goodbye, goodbye, our little table,
nevertheless for us so large.
One takes up — one can hardly believe it —
so little room when pressed close…
Goodbye, our little table!
Just one glass was ours;
each of us, drinking,
sought there the other's lips…
Ah! Poor friend, how he loved me!
Goodbye, our little table, goodbye.

Manon is Massenet's most popular work, and was the opera Puccini had to compete with when he used the same story for his own *Manon Lescaut* several years later (CD 1, Track 9). The plot, though more ornate and including deeper motivations for the main characters, is essentially the same, but the title character, which Massenet has written for a lightish soprano, is even more finely drawn.

This is the moment in the opera after Manon's cousin has convinced her to leave her lover, Des Grieux, for a wealthy benefactor, and she has agreed. Left alone, she acknowledges the sadness of the situation and bids tender farewell to the little table that symbolizes the simple life, the simple happiness and the love they shared.

This type of sentimentality is rare in Callas's package of arias, but late in her career she included it in recitals. Perhaps that is because it sits low and calls for little vocal stress. In any case,

Giuseppe di Stefano, Maria, and Robert Sutherland during the "Farewell Tour," Carnegie Hall, 1974.

given how little it suits either her temperament or her vocal state at the time, there is still much to admire in her interpretation.

In the opening recitative (the first minute), Manon upbraids herself for her own weakness and ponders her happy past and uncertain future. Fittingly, Callas begins in an almost-strong self-recrimination and ends with a fine trailing away which presages the inevitable sadness to come. As she starts the "farewell" (1:00), the sense of intimacy she brings to the moment by the "tiny-ing" of her tone is marvelous. She restates the "adieu" (2:02) amazingly even more intimately than earlier, and the sense of loss she brings to "*Ah! pauvre ami, comme il m'aimait!*" – "Ah, poor friend, how he loved me!" (2:35–2:49) leading up to the final "*Adieu!*" sung as if on a sigh, is immensely moving. Both this aria and Chimène's, before it, are about loss, but Callas never generalized; the characters are different, the scope of their grief is different, therefore, their sounds are different. Even at this stage in her career, with the voice often in fragile condition, the art remained.

TRACK 11: SPONTINI
O NUME TUTELAR (LA VESTALE)

GIULIA

O Nume tutelar degli infelici,
Latona, odi I miei prieghi.
L'ultimo voto mio ti mova, o Nume.
Pria che al destino io soccomba,
fa che dalla mia tomba
s'allontani quell'adorato oggetto
per cui morte m'attende.

GIULIA

O goddess of unhappy wretches,
O Latona, hear my prayers;
let my last prayer move thee, O goddess.
Before I go to meet my fate,
grant that the one
for whom I die
may escape from this tomb.

Gaspare Spontini (1774–1851), though practically forgotten today, is often referred to as "the father of grand opera." Like Gluck, he was a Classicist, but he was also interested in extravagant stagings, great pageantry, large choruses, and in expanding the orchestra—both in size and in range of use. His melodies flow, and despite the old-fashioned quality of his plots and presentation, *La vestale*, his finest work, is worth hearing.

Set in Rome, the plot concerns the vestal virgin, Giulia, and a Roman general. Distracted by her love for him, she allows the Temple's sacred flame to go out; for this she is condemned to be buried alive. In this aria, Giulia, having confessed her sin and prepared for her fate, prays to the Goddess that her beloved not be punished. Divine intervention rekindles the flame, she is pardoned, freed from her vows, and reunited with the Roman general.

The opera had been out of La Scala's repertoire for 25 years when, in 1955, Callas asked that it be brought back for her. A lavish new production was mounted and the five performances she sang were an enormous success. Outside of the opera itself, the only time Callas sang this aria seems to have been for this recording.

The aria is a brief prayer, direct and supplicating. The piety with which she asks the goddess to hear her in the first 45 seconds is both simple and devout; her dip into chest voice on the word "*soccomba*" – "succumb" (1:05) is submissive. Thinking about her loved one (1:23–1:30) brings a softer, more feminine color, and the entirely different manner in which she repeats her plea that her beloved escape her fate (1:59 to the end) is an exquisite show of her love for him. This two-and-a-half minutes embody the crux of Giulia; a vivid portrait.

Maria as Giulia in Spontini's La Vestale, *staged at La Scala in 1954. This was her first time working with the young director Luchino Visconti, the son of a wealthy Milanese nobleman. It was also Visconti's directing debut.*

TRACK 12: BELLINI
AH! NON CREDEA MIRARTI (LA SONNAMBULA)

AMINA

Ah! non credea mirarti
sì presto estinto, o fiore,
passasti al par d'amore,
che un giorno solo durò.
Potria novel vigore
il pianto mio ridarti…
Ma ravvivar l'amore
il pianto mio non può.

AMINA

I hadn't thought I'd see you
dear flower, perished so soon.
You died as did our love
that only lived for a day.
If only my weeping could
restore your strength again…
But all my tears can never
bring back his love to me.

La sonnambula is Bellini's loveliest, most pastoral opera. The gentle heroine, Amina, was another of Giuditta Pasta's creations (along with Norma), and early audiences were, according to composer Mikhail Glinka, driven "to tears of emotion and ecstasy."

The questionable, indeed, inconsequential, plot unfolds in Switzerland, where Amina is betrothed to Elvino. Unbeknownst to everyone, Amina sleepwalks, and when she is found in the room of a visiting Count, she is denounced as an adultress and the wedding is called off. Jealousies and intrigues emerge, but Elvino remains unconvinced. Suddenly, the town notices Amina walking precipitously across a bridge, clearly asleep. She sings this aria (still sleeping) when she reaches safety. She awakens, is given her ring by Elvino, and to general rejoicing, heads for the church to get married.

Callas, despite a clear lack of coyness or girl-ishness in her own dealings, found in Amina's wronged innocence and vindication something to relate to. She sang the role 22 times in two-and-a-half years, and wisely dropped it when her voice and demeanor became too mature. This was recorded in 1955.

To analyze its five minutes seems unnecessary; it's really enough to say that Callas manages to express sadness and hopelessness while also sounding as if she's asleep. She achieves this state of suspension by refusing to alter her tone; it is absolutely even, and her spinning of Bellini's gorgeous, long melodies is an object lesson in bel canto singing.

The entire text is eight lines long. In the first four, Amina holds a bunch of wilted flowers and compares them to her love, which lived only for a day; in the second four, she wishes her weeping could bring them, and Elvino's love, back to life. Lines and thoughts are repeated,

Maria as Amina in a production of Bellini's La sonnambula. *In her early career, Maria said, "I dedicated myself to bel canto roles, to do good for the voice." La Scala, 1956.*

but the simplicity remains. The first one-and-a-half minutes constitute one long melody, the first thought; Callas seems to sing it in one breath. In the second melody, for the lines about weeping (2:23); the first time a word is held longer than the natural rhythm is "*piano*" – "tears" (2:58-3:04), which, of course, deserves greater emphasis. From then on words are repeated in a long, exquisite section for voice and solo cello; after a brief cadenza, the melody is resolved. This aria is magical, a frozen moment of almost unbearable tenderness.

TRACK 13: DONIZETTI
IL DOLCE SUONO MI COLPI DI SUA VOCE!
(LUCIA DI LAMMERMOOR)

LUCIA
Il dolce suono
mi colpì di sua voce!...Ah, quella voce
m'è qui nel cor discesa!
Edgardo, io ti son resa,

LUCIA
I was stirred
by the sweet sound of his voice! Ah, that
  voice
won this heart of mine!

Edgardo, ah, Edgardo mio!

Si, ti son resa,
fuggita io son da' tuoi nemici.
Un gelo mi serpeggia nel sen!
Trema ogni fibra!…Vacilla il piè!
Presso la fonte meco t'assidi alquanto.
Ohimè! Sorge il tremendo
fantasma, e ne separa! Ohimè!
Ohimè! Edgardo! Edgardo! Ah!
Il fantasma ne separa!
Qui ricovriamo, Edgardo, a piè dell'ara.

Sparsa è di rose!…Un' armonia celeste,
dì, non ascolit? Ah! L'inno
suona di nozze! Il rito
per noi s'appresta!…O me felice!
Edgardo, Edgardo, oh me felice!
O, gioia che si sente e non si dice!
Ardon gl'incensi…splendon
le sacre faci, splendon intorno!
Ecco il Ministro! Porgimi
la destra…Oh, lieto giorno!
Alfin son tua, alfin sei mio,
a me ti dona un Dio.

Edgardo, I am yours again,
Edgardo, ah, my Edgardo!
Yes, I am yours again,
I have flown from your enemies.
An icy shiver creeps in my bosom.
Every nerve quivers! My step falters!
Sit with me a while near the fountain.
Alas! The terrible spectre rises
and parts us! Alas!
Alas! Edgardo! Edgardo! Ah!
The spectre…parts us!
Here let us hide, Edgardo, at the foot of the
    altar.
It is strewn with roses! Celestial harmony,
do you not hear it? Ah, strains
of our wedding-hymn! The ceremony
awaits us!…Oh, how happy I am!
Edgardo, Edgardo, how happy I am!
Oh, joy that I feel but cannot express!
The incense is burning — the sacred
torches are glowing all around!
Here is the minister! Give me
your hand…Oh, happy day!
At last I am yours, at last you are mine,
God has given you to me.

Lucia di Lammermoor is Donizetti's most famous opera. Its emotions are raw, confrontation scenes affecting in the best sense, and in a good performance, the excitement runs very high. All of that aside, in the first half of the twentieth century, wherever there was a box-office-savvy impresario and a coloratura soprano who wished to show off her staccati, agility and high notes, there was a production of *Lucia*. The Mad Scene (recorded here), which includes sections in which the soprano's voice is preceded or accompanied by a flute playing the same melody or a complementary one, is an astonishing feat.

Taken from a story by Sir Walter Scott, the

Maria as Lucia in the "Mad Scene," La Scala, 1954.

opera tells of a young lady (Lucia) forced into a loveless marriage for political reasons by her brother after he has convinced her that the man she really loves (Edgardo) has abandoned her. After the marriage, she slashes her husband to death. In the scene recorded here, after the murder has been discovered, Lucia enters, bloodied and insane, relives moments in her past, hallucinates, imagines her wedding is to Edgardo, and finally, after wishing that he might weep for her on earth and join her in heaven, she collapses.

It is not overstating the case to say that Lucia had become little other than a showcase for a soprano with bell-like tones until Callas came along. At the opera's earliest performances, audience members wept at Lucia's plight; by the 1940s, audiences sat politely and waited for the coloratura acrobatics, culminating in what had better turn out to be a perfectly placed high E-flat.

There are three Callas recordings of the complete opera on EMI; this is taken from a live performance under conductor Herbert von Karajan, in Berlin in 1955. Often acknowledged to be the pinnacle of her career, its spontaneity, drama and gorgeous singing are reason enough for the invention of recording equipment.

The scene is in sections: Lucia's entrance, with a background flute suggesting her mental chaos, has her gently recalling the voice ("*Il dolce suono*" – "The sweet sound") of Edgardo; that thought is violently interrupted by the disjointed, fearful memory ("*Un gelo mi serpeggia nel sen*" – "A chill runs through my body") of the fountain at which she used to meet Edgardo and the ghost which arose from it ("*Ahimè! sorge il tremendo fantasma*" – Oh! A terrible spectre rises). Her thoughts wander again and she imagines herself and Edgardo at an altar, about to marry. She's carried away by gentle contentment: She pictures the ceremony ("*Ardon gl' incensi*" – "The incense is burning"), the candles and the priest, and she expresses her happiness. It is at this point that the hallucination becomes wordless, a lengthy cadenza accompanied by flute, filled with coloratura fireworks; Donizetti did not write the cadenza, it is left to the discretion and abilities of the soprano and invariably ends with an interpolated high note. Then comes the final section (Track 14), a verse and variations ("*Spargi d'amaro pianto*" – "Spread with bitter tears [my earthly remains]") with more fireworks, another ultimate stratospheric note, and her collapse.

The tone Callas uses to begin "*Il dolce suono*" is as sweet as the thought, and it's clear from the start that we're dealing with a fragile, delicate, abused creature. The tone has a far-away aspect to it; Callas puts no pressure on the voice at the start. At the mention of Edgardo's name the tone is heavier (0:59), and it is emphasized each time (1:11 ff). Through these subtle gradations of tone we see the sadness beneath the lunacy. At "I have flown from your enemies" (1:39), the voice takes wing, but the sadness remains. Describing the chill creeping through her body, we get the type of verbal nuance on "*serpeggia*" – "creeps" (2:05), which tells it all. This woman is one exposed nerve ending; every tiny feeling affects her deeply. At "*vacilla al piè*" (2:23) as she's losing her footing, we realize that her physical equilibrium is off as well. Her invitation to Edgardo to sit with her at the fountain is calm.

Then something happens that throws her into a mental spasm. At "*Ohimè!*" (3:25), she imagines the ghost and calls out to Edgardo; her repetition of the word "*fantasma*" – "ghost" is dark, terrified (3:42), the voice of one possessed, totally different from what has come

before it. Sudden shifts in tempo and volume are, of course, written by the composer; the shift in shade and temperament must come from a voice with gradations of tone and a complete identification with the character. There is a sudden shift again at "*Qui ricovriamo, Edgardo,*" when Lucia invites Edgardo to hide at the altar; there's a lovely, light flourish to express the momentary peace and happiness she feels (3:56–4:21). Lucia continues in a steady vein, visualizing the altar strewn with roses, hearing the wedding hymn: Are the repeated cries of "*Ah, Ah, Ah!*" (5:13ff) happy or insane? While Lucia claims to be happy, the tone gives her away. She calls out to Edgardo again twice, followed by a more manic, fuller-voiced grand vocal gesture with a cadenza up to high C and back ending on a tragic, false expression of joy – "*O me felice!*" (5:37–5:57). She claims she can't express her joy; it is, of course, not joy, but mental chaos. As she expresses "inexpressible" joy in the text, the voice goes up and down scales; the sense is of anything but joy (6:01 ff).

At "*Ardon gl'incensi*" (6:40 ff), the little, happy-girl voice returns. Lucia is play-acting. On "*O lieto giorno, o lieto*" (7:21 ff) the tone is anything but "*lieto*" – "happy," and when, she exclaims "*Alfin son tua*" – "At last, I'm yours" (7:41 ff) the sound is heavy and sad: "finally" apparently wasn't soon enough. She play-acts the happiness again (the chorus interjects, commenting on her plight; 8:26 ff), fantasizing that she's sharing her pleasure with Edgardo. But the voice is heavy, worn out, exhausted. At "*Del ciel clemente*" (9:20) we hear total defeat. Despite what she says, it is obvious that Heaven has shown *no* mercy. "Our life will be a smile together," is repeated until her mania takes over entirely. The flute begins to mirror her broken mind. It is here that the cadenza begins; words have failed her, only sounds come out (10:24 ff). This is a display of simply astonishing vocal acrobatics, totally secure singing of staccati, turns, runs up and down octaves. Then, at the penul-timate moment, there's some vocal suspense before the normally taken high E-flat. Callas instead holds the high B-flat forte, diminishes it (12:04–12:20), then dips to low E-flat. As we realize at the end of the next section, this is not because Callas does not have the note at her command: she is demonstrating the defeat Lucia is feeling. Not many sopranos would have the nerve to make such a choice, and it can anger an audience.

Maria as Lucia, La Scala, 1954. Her performance in the role the following year in Berlin is considered by many to be the definitive Lucia of her career.

TRACK 14: DONIZETTI
SPARGI D'AMARO PIANTO (LUCIA DI LAMMERMOOR)

LUCIA

Spargi d'amaro pianto
il mio terrestre velo,
mentre lassù nel cielo
io pregherò per te.
Al giunger tuo soltanto,
fia bello il ciel per me,
ah sì, per me, ecc.

RAIMONDO e CORO

Più raffrenare il pianto
possibile non è, ecc.

ENRICO

Giorni d'amaro pianto
serba il rimorso a me, ecc.

LUCIA

Ah! spargi d'amaro pianto, ecc.

LUCIA

Shed bitter tears
on my earthly garment,
while in Heaven above
I will pray for you.
Only when you join me,
will Heaven be blissful for me,
ah yes, for me, etc.

RAIMONDO and CHORUS

It is impossible
to hold back the tears, etc.

ENRICO

Remorse will bring me
days of bitter weeping, etc.

LUCIA

Ah! shed bitter tears, etc.

Following immediately on the heels of the nerve-wracking cadenza, Lucia sings the first verse of her final requests close to uninflectedly (0:28 ff); she sounds almost relieved to have gotten the outburst out of her system and she merely wants to finish her life. Note the beautiful trills (starting at 1:12) and the gorgeous, filigreed passage work which follows. In the repeat of the verse, after the choral interruption (2:02 ff) she embellishes the vocal line, with a flourish on "*velo*" (2:26) and some stunning staccati. After asking heaven to be joyful for her, she repeats "I will pray for you [Edgardo]" on the word "*te*" – "you" (2:40–2:49) she draws the note and word out, from a B-flat up to an almost dead-sounding B (though right on pitch, in utter control). From there to the end, she sounds almost positive as she repeats that heaven will be a joy for her, absolutely focused on her final moments on earth. She ends on an astonishing, triumphant high E-flat, rock-solid and the last note we ever hear from Lucia.

Needless to say, performed magnificently, the Mad Scene takes the listener through as many mood changes as Lucia goes through, and never more so than in Callas's hands. Great coloratura sopranos can _sing_ all the music; Callas sings it superbly, but there's so much more: Smooth declarations contrasted with emotional eruptions, control over dynamics from the lightest to the heaviest, fearless delivery of the most difficult music, careful attention to the text, and the ability to make the vocal acrobatics an integral part of Lucia's madness rather than empty showmanship. These all add up to something miraculous.

Being "mad" is not generic: Compare Lucia with Lady Macbeth, Dinorah or Anna Bolena. Being in love is not generic: Gilda is not Juliette, nor is she Lauretta. Being sad is not generic: Tosca cannot be compared with Wally or Violetta or Chimène; Orphée is different still. Even the manners in which Dalila and Carmen seduce differ. These, and the other characters she portrayed, through Callas's artistry, her mind and sensibility, are individuals. This is what made Callas Callas.

Glossary

Acciaccatura—a type of embellishment: the note above the main note sung almost at the same time (actually a split second before) and released immediately.

Appoggiatura—a type of embellishment: a slow single note, a grace note, sung immediately following the main note.

Aria—like a soliloquy in music, a solo song in an opera.

Bel canto—literally defined as "beautiful singing," it is far more complicated. It implies not only a beauty of tone but expertise in all aspects of singing—breath control, portamento, legato, to name three. Those versed in the art of bel canto indulge in an overt emotionalism which nevertheless must never mar the sung line. In brief, it is a concentration on melody in conjunction with vocal prowess to communicate and define character.

Cadenza—a brilliant solo at the discretion of the performer, typically a chance to display his or her technical prowess, usually at the end of an aria or scene.

Castrato—male singer castrated before puberty to keep the voice high, while possessing the power and chest cavity of a man.

Chest register—the lower part of the voice, below the "head" voice or falsetto; the tones produce sympathetic vibrations in the chest cavity.

Coloratura—term encompassing vocal agility, nimbleness, light delivery of passages adding to the brilliancy of a composition and displaying the singer's skill.

Dramatic Soprano—a dark, heavy soprano, one whose voice is capable of riding over a large orchestra.

Embellishment—a tradition of alterations the performer can make to the score, including trills, runs and alternate notes.

Fioriture—ornamentation, or embellishment introduced into a melody.

Forte, fortissimo—loud, louder.

Legato—smooth, connected movement between notes.

Lyric soprano—a light, focused soprano voice, easily produced, not required or expected to carry over a large orchestra, nor expected to sing in a very high range.

Melisma—more than one note per syllable,

sometimes quite elaborate ornamentation (see also embellishing, coloratura).

Piano, pianissimo—soft, softer.

Pitch—the position of a note on a musical scale; the note.

Portamento—an elegant "slide" between notes, more "conscious" and emphatic than legato; all of the notes in between can be heard, however quickly.

Recitative—operatic moments that are close to accompanied speech, usually used to advance a plot or before an aria, to set the stage for that aria.

Roulade—embellishment, vocal flourish (French).

Scale—the stepwise series of notes that define a specific key. The bottom note is the name of the key (C major scale, in the key of C, has as its first note a C). When it is said that a singer is practicing or singing scales, it means he or she is vocalizing up and down a series of notes.

Staccato—short, abrupt attacks on notes; the opposite of legato.

Timbre—the "color" of a note, meaning the quality of the sound and not just the pitch.

Tone—1) a note, 2) the quality of a note.

Trill—even, rapid alternation between two notes; sometimes an additional effect added by the singer. A type of embellishment.

Chronology

1923

2 December: Maria Anna Sophia Cecilia Kalogeropoulou is born in New York. Her parents, Evangelia and George Kalogeropoulos, had emigrated from Greece to Long Island, New York, in August 1923.

1929

George Kalogeropoulos sets up a pharmacy in a Greek quarter of Manhattan; he changes the family name to Callas.

1932

Maria is given her first piano lessons; later in life she is able to study all her roles at the piano without the help of a repetiteur.

1937

The parents separate. Evangelia returns to Greece with her two daughters and changes the family name back to Kalogeropoulos.

1938

Maria Kalogeropoulou is admitted to the National Conservatory in Athens despite being below the minimum age requirement of 16; she begins her studies under Maria Trivella.

11 April: Appears with fellow students in first public recital.

1939

2 April: Maria makes her stage debut as Santuzza, in a student production of *Cavalleria rusticana*, and wins the Conservatory's prize.

Elvira de Hidalgo becomes Maria's teacher and concentrates on coloratura training.

1940

21 October: First engagement with the Lyric Theatre company, singing songs in Shakespeare's *Merchant of Venice* at the Royal Theatre in Athens.

1941

21 January: Makes her professional operatic debut as Beatrice in *Boccaccio* at the Palas Cinema, Athens, with the Lyric Theatre company, with whom she will sing in *Tosca*, *Tiefland*, *Cavalleria rusticana*, *Fidelio*, *O Protomastoras*, *Boccaccio*, and *Der Bettelstudent* over the next four years.

1942

27 August: Sings Tosca for the first time in Greek at an open-air performance at the Park Summer Theatre, Klafthmonos Square.

1944

The occupying forces lose control over Greece; the British fleet arrives in Piraeus. Maria Kalogeropoulou decides to return to the USA and find her father.

1945

3 August: Gives a 'farewell' concert in Athens—her first solo recital—to raise money for her journey to the USA.

September: Returns to New York and takes the name of Callas again.

December: Auditions for the Metropolitan Opera but fails to secure an engagement.

1946

Maria tries unsuccessfully to find work while continuing strenuous vocal practice to perfect her technique; meets agent Eddie Bagarozy. Accepts an engagement to sing in *Turandot* in Chicago in January 1947 with cast of celebrated European singers in a new company to be founded by Bagarozy together with Ottavio Scotto, an Italian impresario.

1947

January: The Chicago company goes bankrupt a few days before its scheduled opening peformance. A member of the company (the Italian bass Nicola Rossi-Lemeni) introduces Callas to Giovanni Zenatello, who is in the USA to find singers for the 1947 Verona Opera Festival; he engages Callas to sing in *La Gioconda*.

27 June: Callas arrives in Naples and goes the next day to Verona to begin rehearsals; a few days later she meets Giovanni Battista Meneghini, a wealthy Italian industrialist and opera-lover.

2 August: Makes her Italian debut in the Arena at Verona in *La Gioconda* conducted by Tullio Serafin. The performances are successful enough but Callas makes no special impression and

expected offers of further work do not materialise.

30 December: Sings Isolde in Italian under Serafin at La Fenice in Venice; this leads to further engagements in Italy, mainly in *Turandot*.

1948

30 November: In Florence, Callas sings Norma for the first time: this is the role she will eventually perform more than any other during her career.

1949

19 January: Having just sung her first Brünnhilde in *Die Walküre* eleven days earlier, Callas, at the insistence of Serafin, replaces the indisposed Margherita Carosio as Elvira in *I puritani* at La Fenice. The opera world is stunned by her performance. This is the turning point in Callas's career and the start of her involvement in the rehabilitation of the Italian bel canto repertoire.

21 April: Marries Meneghini in Verona and sails that night for Argentina to sing at the Teatro Colon in Buenos Aires.

With Meneghini's help as both husband and manager, Callas develops her career in Italy and abroad during the next two years.

1951

7 December: Callas opens the season at La Scala, Milan in *I vespri siciliani* to great acclaim; over the next seven years La Scala will be the scene of her greatest triumphs in a wide range of roles.

1952

29 July: Callas signs recording contract with EMI.

1953

February: First commercial recording for EMI is *Lucia di Lammermoor*, recorded in Florence.

Later in the year: Callas begins a series of complete opera recordings at La Scala: *I puritani* and *Cavalleria rusticana* conducted by Serafin are followed by *Tosca* under Victor de Sabata.

1954

Callas reduces her weight by 30 kilos and her appearance changes dramatically. She records a further four complete operas at La Scala and her first two recital discs in London.

November: She returns to the USA to sing in *Norma*, *La traviata* and *Lucia di Lammermoor* in Chicago.

December: She opens the season at La Scala in *La Vestale*, working for the first time with theatre and film director Luchino Visconti.

1956

29 October: Sings for the first time at the Metropolitan, New York, in *Norma*, followed by *Tosca* and *Lucia*.

1957

2 January: Pleading illness, Callas withdraws after the first act of a gala performance of Norma in Rome, attended by the President of Italy and all of Rome society; she is harshly criticized in the media.

May: At La Scala, during performances of *Il pirata*, she quarrels with general director Antonio Ghiringhelli, and decides not to appear again at La Scala while he remains in charge.

September: Elsa Maxwell, the American society hostess, introduces the Meneghinis to the Greek shipping magnate Aristotle Onassis at a party in Venice.

6 November: Rudolf Bing, director of the Metropolitan Opera, fires Callas after failing to reach an agreement with her on performances for the next season.

19 December: She makes a sensational debut in Paris in a gala concert at the Paris Opera; celebrities in the audience include Onassis, who begins to take a closer interest in Callas.

1959

By this time Callas has fewer professional engagements. She and Meneghini are invited for a cruise in July on Onassis's yacht, the *Christina*, with several other guests including the Churchills; by the end of the cruise Callas and Onassis are lovers and the Meneghini marriage is over.

1960–63

Callas curtails her stage appearances and devotes herself to the international high life with Onassis; by 1962 she gives just the occasional concert.

1964

January: Franco Zeffirelli persuades Callas to return to opera at Covent Garden in a memorable new production of *Tosca* that is highly praised.

May: Callas appears in Paris in *Norma*, directed by Zeffirelli, in a spectacular staging that is to be her last new production. Despite some vocal problems, the performances are successful overall.

1965

February: She sings nine performances of *Tosca* in Paris.

March: She makes a triumphant return to the Metropolitan in New York in two performances of *Tosca*.

May: She undertakes another five performances of *Norma* in Paris. Feeling tired but determined to fulfill the engagement, she can barely finish Act II, Scene 1 on May 29th. The final scene is cancelled.

July: She is scheduled to sing four performances of *Tosca* at Covent Garden. Advised to withdraw on medical grounds, she decides to sing just once; she chooses the Royal Gala on July 5th, which turns out to be her final appearance on the operatic stage.

1966

Callas relinquishes her American citizenship and takes Greek nationality, thereby technically annulling her marriage to Meneghini; she expects Onassis to marry her but he does not.

1968

20 October: After cooling his relationship with Callas, Onassis marries Jacqueline Kennedy, widow of assassinated U.S. president John F. Kennedy; Callas is devastated.

1969

June–July: Callas plays Medea in a non-musical film of the play by Euripides, directed by Pier Paolo Pasolini. It is not a commercial success.

1971-72

Callas gives a series of master classes at the Juilliard School of Music in New York. She meets up again with her old colleague, the tenor Giuseppe di Stefano, and the two become close friends.

1973

Di Stefano persuades Callas to undertake an extensive international recital tour with him. The tour, a personal triumph but an artistic failure, begins in Hamburg on October 25th and continues into 1974.

1974

11 November: The final concert of the tour with di Stefano takes place in Sapporo, Japan: this is Callas's last public performance.

1975

15 March: Onassis dies after an operation; Callas is by now a virtual recluse in Paris.

1977

16 September: Alone in her apartment, Callas dies of natural causes.

Performance History

OPERAS

OPERA	LOCATION	CONDUCTOR
D'ALBERT		
Tiefland – about 11 performances		
First: 22 April 1944	Athens	Zoras
Last: 24 March 1945	Athens	Zoras
BEETHOVEN		
Fidelio – about 6 performances (in Greek)		
First: 14 August 1944	Herodes Atticus, Athens	Hoerner or Zoras
Last: ? August 1944	Herodes Atticus, Athens	Hoerner or Zoras
BELLINI		
Norma – 92 performances		
First: 30 November 1948	Florence	Serafin
Last: 29 May 1965	Paris	Prêtre
Il pirata – 7 performances		
First: 19 May 1958	La Scala, Milan	Votto
Last: 29 January 1959	Washington (concert)	Rescigno
I puritani – 16 performances		
First: 19 January 1949	Venice	Serafin
Last: 2 November 1955	Chicago	Rescigno
La sonnambula – 22 performances		
First: 5 March 1955	La Scala, Milan	Bernstein
Last: 29 August 1957	Edinburgh Festival	Votto

BOITO

Mefistofele – 3 performances

First: 15 July 1954	Verona	Votto
Last: 25 July 1954	Verona	Votto

CHERUBINI

Medea – 31 performances

First: 7 May 1953	Florence	Gui
Last: 3 June 1962	La Scala, Milan	Schippers

DONIZETTI

Anna Bolena – 12 performances

First: 14 April 1957	La Scala, Milan	Gavazzeni
Last: 23 April 1958	La Scala, Milan	Votto

Lucia di Lammermoor – 46 performances

First: 10 June 1952	Mexico City	Picco
Last: 8 November 1959	Dallas	Rescigno

Poliuto – 5 performances

First: 7 December 1960	La Scala, Milan	Votto
Last: 21 December 1960	La Scala, Milan	Votto

GIORDANO

Andrea Chénier – 6 performances

First: 8 January 1955	La Scala, Milan	Votto
Last: 6 February 1955	La Scala, Milan	Votto

Fedora – 6 performances

First: 21 May 1956	La Scala, Milan	Gavazzeni
Last: 3 June 1956	La Scala, Milan	Gavazzeni

GLUCK

Alceste – 4 performances

First: 4 April 1954	La Scala, Milan	Giulini
Last: 20 April 1954	La Scala, Milan	Giulini

Iphigénie en Tauride – 4 performances

First: 1 June 1957	La Scala, Milan	Sanzogno
Last: 10 June 1957	La Scala, Milan	Sanzogno

HAYDN

Orfeo ed Euridice – 2 performances

First: 9 June 1951	Florence	Kleiber
Last: 10 June 1951	Florence	Kleiber

KALOMIRIS

O Promastoras – 2 performances

First: July 1944	Herodes Atticus, Athens	Kalomiris
Last: 5 August 1944	Herodes Atticus, Athens	Kalomiris

MASCAGNI

Cavalleria rusticana – about 6 performances (in Greek)

First: 2 April 1939	Athens	Bourtsis (piano)
Last: 9 May 1944	Athens	Karalivanos

MILLÖCKER

Der Betelstudent – about 4 performances (in Greek)

First: 5 September 1945	Athens	Evanghelatos
Last: ? September 1945	Athens	Evanghelatos

MOZART

Die Entführung aus dem Serail – 4 performances (in Italian)

First: 2 April 1952	La Scala , Milan	Perlea
Last: 9 April 1952	La Scala, Milan	Perlea

PONCHIELLI

La Gioconda – 13 performances

First: 2 August 1947	Verona	Serafin
Last: 19 February 1953	La Scala, Milan	Votto

PUCCINI

Madama Butterfly – 3 performances

First: 11 November 1955	Chicago	Rescigno
Last: 17 November 1955	Chicago	Rescigno

Tosca – about 37 performances (first few in Greek)

First: 27 August 1942	Athens	Vasiliadis
Last: 5 July 1965	Covent Garden, London	Prêtre

Turandot — 24 performances

First: 29 January 1948	Venice	Sanzogno
Last: 22 June 1949	Buenos Aires	Serafin

ROSSINI

Armida — 3 performances

First: 26 April 1952	Florence	Serafin
Last: 4 May 1952	Florence	Serafin

Il barbiere di Siviglia — 5 performances

First: 16 February 1956	La Scala, Milan	Giulini
Last: 15 March 1956	La Scala, Milan	Giulini

Il turco in Italia — 9 performances

First: 19 October 1950	Rome	Gavazzeni
Last: 4 May 1955	La Scala, Milan	Gavazzeni

SPONTINI

La Vestale — 5 performances

First: 7 December 1954	La Scala, Milan	Votto
Last: 18 December 1954	La Scala, Milan	Votto

SUPPÉ

Boccaccio — about 18 performances (in Greek)

First: 21 January 1941	Athens	Pfeffer or Zoras
Last: ? July 1941	Athens	Pfeffer or Zoras

VERDI

Aida — 33 performances

First: 18 September 1948	Turin	Serafin
Last: 8 August 1953	Verona	Ghione

Un ballo in maschera — 5 performances

First: 7 December 1957	La Scala, Milan	Gavazzeni
Last: 22 December 1957	La Scala, Milan	Gavazzeni

Don Carlo — 5 performances

First: 12 April 1954	La Scala, Milan	Votto
Last: 27 April 1954	La Scala, Milan	Votto

La forza del destino – 6 performances
First: 17 April 1948   Trieste   Parenti
Last: 26 May 1954   Ravenna   Ghione

Macbeth – 5 performances
First: 7 December 1952   La Scala, Milan   De Sabata
Last: 17 December 1952   La Scala, Milan   De Sabata

Nabucco – 3 performances
First: 20 December 1949   Naples   Gui
Last: 27 December 1949   Naples   Gui

Rigoletto – 2 performances
First: 17 June 1952   Mexico City   Mugnai
Last: 21 June 1952   Mexico City   Mugnai

La traviata – 63 performances
First: 14 January 1951   Florence   Serafin
Last: 2 November 1958   Dallas   Rescigno

Il trovatore – 20 performances
First: 20 June 1950   Mexico City   Picco
Last: 8 November 1955   Chicago   Rescigno

I vespri siciliani – 11 performances
First: 26 May 1951   Florence   Kleiber
Last: 3 January 1952   La Scala   Quadri

WAGNER
Parsifal – 4 performances (in Italian)
First: 26 February 1949   Rome   Serafin
Last: 8 March 1949   Rome   Serafin

Tristan und Isolde – 12 performances (in Italian)
First: 30 December 1947   Venice   Serafin
Last: 28 February 1950   Rome   Serafin

Die Walküre – 6 performances (in Italian)
First: 8 January 1949   Venice   Serafin
Last: 10 February 1949   Palermo   Molinari Pradelli

CONCERTS

DATE	LOCATION	REPERTOIRE:
October, 1942	Salonika	Rossini arias, duets and songs
April 22, 1943	Athens	Music Unknown
July 21, 1943	Mousouri	*Atalanta* and excerpts from *Cenerentola*, *Adriana Lecouvreur*, and *Trovatore*
August 2, 1943	Salonika	Rossini arias
August 3, 1943	Salonika	Leider by Schubert and Brahms
September 26, 1943	Athens	Excerpts from *Fidelio*, *Aida* and arias by Thaïs Mozart and Turina
December 12, 1943	Athens	Excerpts from *Fidelio*, *Semiramide*, *Trovatore*, and arias by Turina
May 21, 1944	Athens	'Casta Diva' from *Norma*
October, 1944	Salonika	Concert for troops, music unknown
March 20, 1945	Athens	Arias by Ronald and Vaughan Williams
August 3, 1945	Athens	Excerpts from *Don Giovanni*, *Semiramide*, *Aida*, *Trovatore*, *Oberon* and songs by Granados, Kariotaki and Poniridi.
March 7, 1949	Turin	Excerpts from *Tristan und Isolde*, *Norma*, *Puritani*, and *Aida*
July 9, 1949	Buenos Aires	*Norma* and *Turandot*
March 13, 1950	Turin	Excerpts from *Oberon*, *Traviata*, *Trovatore*, and *Dinorah*
March, 12, 1951	Turin	Excerpts from *Ballo*, *Mignon*, and *Freischütz*
April 21, 1951	Trieste	Excerpts from *Norma*, *Puritani*, *Aida* and *Traviata*
June 11, 1951	Florence	Excerpts from *Norma*, *Dinorah*, *Aida*, *Mignon*, *Traviata*, and variations by Proch on 'Deh torna mio ben'
July 15, 1951	Mexico City	Excerpts from *Forza* and *Ballo*
September 14, 1951	Rio di Janeiro	'Sempre libera,' from *Traviata*
February 18, 1952	Rome	Excerpts from *Macbeth*, *Lucia*, *Nabucco*, and *Lakmé*
December 27, 1954	San Remo	Exerpts from *Entführung*, *Dinorah*, *Louise*, and *Armida*
September 27, 1956	Milan	Excerpts from *Vestale*, *Semiramide*, *Hamlet*, and *Puritani*
December 17, 1956	Washington, D.C.	Excerpts from *Norma*, *Trovatore*, *Traviata*, *Lucia*, and *Tosca*

January 15, 1957	Chicago	Excerpts from *Sonnambula, Dinorah, Turandot, Norma, Trovatore,* and *Lucia*
June 19, 1957	Zurich	Excerpts from *Traviata* and *Lucia*
August 5, 1957	Athens	Excerpts from *Forza, Trovatore, Lucia, Tristan* and *Hamlet*
November 21, 1957	Dallas	Excerpts from *Entführung, Puritani, Macbeth, Traviata* and *Anna Bolena*
January 22, 1958	Chicago	Excerpts from *Don Giovanni, Macbeth, Barbiere, Mefistofele, Nabucco, Hamlet*
March 24, 1958	Madrid	Excerpts from *Norma, Trovatore, Mefistofele,* and *Hamlet*

"1958–1959 Tour"

October 11, 1958	Birmingham	Excerpts from *Vestale, Macbeth, Barbiere, Mefistofele, Bohème,* and *Hamlet*
October 14	Atlanta	
October, 17	Montreal	
October, 21	Toronto	
November, 15	Cleveland	
November 18	Detroit	
November 22	New York	
November 26	San Francisco	
November 29	Los Angeles	
January 11, 1959	St. Louis	
December 19, 1958	Paris	Excerpts from *Norma, Trovatore, Barbiere,* and *Tosca*
January 24, 1959	Philadelphia	Excerpts from *Mefistofele, Barbiere,* and *Hamlet*
May 2, 1959	Madrid	Excerpts from *Don Giovanni, Macbeth, Semiramide, Gioconda,* and *Pirata*
May 5, 1959	Barcelona	Excerpts from *Don Carlos, Mefistofele, Barbiere, Tosca, Bohème,* and *Pirata*
May 24, 1959	Munich	Excerpts from *Vestale, Macbeth, Barbiere, Don Carlos,* and *Pirata*
July 14, 1959	Brussels	Excerpts from *Vestale, Ernani, Don Carlos,* and *Pirata*
September 17, 1959	Bilbao	Excerpts from *Don Carlos, Hamlet, Ernani,* and *Pirata*
September 23, 1959	London	Excerpts from *Don Carlos, Hamlet, Macbeth,* and *Pirata*
October 23, 1959	Berlin	Excerpts from *Don Giovanni, Ernani, Don Carlos,* and *Hamlet*
October 28, 1959	Kansas City	Excerpts from *Don Giovanni, Lucia, Ernani,* and *Pirata*

May 30, 1961	London	Excerpts from *Norma*, *Le Cid*, *Mefistofele*, and *Don Carlos*
February 27, 1962	London	Excerpts from *Don Carlos*, *Le Cid*, *Cenerentola*, *Anna Bolena*, *Macbeth*, and *Oberon*

Tour of Germany

March 12, 1962	Munich	Excerpts from *Don Carlos*, *Le Cid*, *Cenerentola*, *Carmen*, and *Ernani*
March 16	Hamburg	
March 19	Essen	
March 23	Bonn	
May 19, 1962	New York, President Kennedy's forty-fourth birthday celebration	Excerpts from *Carmen*
May 17, 1963	Berlin	Excerpts from *Norma*, *Nabucco*, *Bohème*, *Madama Butterfly*, and *Gianni Schicchi*
May 20	Düsseldorf	
May 23	Stuttgart	
May 31	London	
July 9	London	
June 5	Paris	Excerpts from *Semiramide*, *Cenerentola*, *Werther*, *Manon*, *Nabucco*, *Bohème*, *Madama Butterfly*, and *Gianni Schicci*

1973 "Farewell Tour"

October 25	Hamburg	Excerpts from *Le Cid*, *Carmen*, *Gioconda*,
October 29	Berlin	*Mefistofele*, *Don Carlos*, *Gianni Schicchi*,
November 2	Düsseldorf	*Bohème*, *Faust*, *Elisir*, *Forza*, *Cavalleria*, *Vespri*,
November 6	Munich	*Manon Lescaut*, *Werther*, *Tosca*, and *Manon*
November 9	Frankfurt	
November 12	Mannheim	
November 20	Madrid	
November 26,		
December 2	London	
December 8	Paris	
December 11	Amsterdam	

$\mathcal{D}$iscography

COMPLETE OPERAS

BELLINI

Norma (1954) – Filippeschi, Stignani, Rossi-Lemeni/Coro e Orchestra del Teatro alla Scala di Milano/Tullio Serafin (3 CDs 5 56271 2)

Norma (2nd version, 1960) – Corelli, Zaccaria, Ludwig/Coro e Orchestra del Teatro alla Scala di Milano/Tullio Serafin (3 CDs 5 66428 2)

Il pirata (live recording, New York, 1959) – Ferraro, Ego/Chorus and Orchestra of the American Opera Society/Nicola Rescigno (2 CDs 5 66432 2)

I puritani (1953) – Di Stefano, Rossi-Lemeni, Panerai/Coro e Orchestra del Teatro alla Scala di Milano/Tullio Serafin (2 CDs 5 56275 2)

La sonnambula (1957) – Zaccaria, Cossotto, Moni/Coro e Orchestra del Teatro alla Scala di Milano/Antonino Votto (2 CDs 5 56278 2)

BIZET

Carmen (1964) – Gedda, Guiot, Massard/Chœurs René Duclos/Orchestre du Théâtre National de l'Opéra/Georges Prêtre (2 CDs 5 56581 2)

DONIZETTI

Anna Bolena (live recording, Milan, 1957) – Simionato, Rossi-Lemeni/Coro e Orchestra del Teatro alla Scala di Milano/Gianandrea Gavazzeni (2 CDs 5 66471 2)

Lucia di Lammermoor (1953) – Di Stefano, Gobbi/Coro e Orchestra del Maggio Musicale Fiorentino/Tullio Serafin (2 CDs 5 66438 2)

Lucia di Lammermoor (second version, 1959) – Tagliavini, Cappuccilli, Ladysz/Philharmonia Orchestra and Chorus/Tullio Serafin (2 CDs 5 56284 2)

Lucia di Lammermoor (live recording, Berlin, 1955) – Di Stefano, Panerai, Zaccaria/Coro del Teatro alla Scala di Milano/RIAS Sinfonie-Orchester Berlin/Herbert von Karajan (2 CDs 5 66441 2)

Poliuto (live recording, Milan, 1960) – Corelli, Bastianini, Zaccaria/Coro e Orchestra del Teatro alla Scala di Milano/Antonio Votto (2 CDs 5 65448 2)

GLUCK

Ifigenia in Tauride (live recording, Milan, 1957) Albanese, Dondi, Colzani, Cossotto/Coro e Orchestra del Teatro alla Scala di Milano/Nino Sanzogno (2 CDs 5 65451 2)

MASCAGNI/LEONCAVALLO

Cavalleria rusticana/Pagliacci (1953, 1954) – Di Stefano, Panerai, Gobbi/Coro e Orchestra del Teatro alla Scala di Milano/Tullio Serafin (2 CDs 5 56287 2)

PONCHIELLI

La Gioconda (1959) – Cossotto, Vinco, Ferraro, Cappuccilli/Coro e Orchestra del Teatro alla Scala di Milano/Antonino Votto (3 CDs 5 56291 2)

PUCCINI

La bohème (1956) – Di Stefano, Panerai, Zaccaria, Moffo/Coro e Orchestra del Teatro alla Scala di Milano/Antonino Votto (2CDs 5 56295 2)

Madama Butterfly (1955) – Gedda, Danieli, Borriello/Coro e Orchestra del Teatro alla Scala di Milano/Herbert von Karajan (2 CDs 5 56298 2)

Manon Lescaut (1957) – Di Stefano, Fioravanti/Coro & Orchestra del Teatro alla Scala di Milano/Tullio Serafin (2 CDs 5 56301 2)

Tosca (1953) – Di Stefano, Gobbi/Coro e Orchestra del Teatro alla Scala di Milano/Victor de Sabata (2 CDs 5 56304 2)

Tosca (2nd version, 1965) – Bergonzi, Gobbi/Chœurs et Orchestre du Théâtre National de l'Opéra/ Georges Prêtre (2 CDs 5 66444 2)

Turandot (1957) – Fernandi, Schwarzkopf, Zaccaria/Coro e Orchestra del Teatro alla Scala di Milano/Tullio Serafin (2 CDs 5 56307 2)

ROSSINI

Il barbiere di Siviglia (1957) – Alva, Gobbi, Zaccaria, Ollendorff/Philharmonia Orchestra and Chorus/Alceo Galliera (2 CDs 5 56310 2)

Il turco in Italia (1954) – Rossi-Lemeni, Gedda, Calabrese/Coro e Orchestra del Teatro alla Scala di Milano/Gianandrea Gavazzeni (2 CDs 5 56313 2)

VERDI

Aida (1955) – Tucker, Barbieri, Gobbi, Zaccaria/Coro e Orchestra del Teatro alla Scala di Milano/Tullio Serafin (2 CDs 5 56316 2)

Un ballo in maschera (1956) – Di Stefano, Gobbi, Barbieri, Ratti/Coro e Orchestra del Teatro alla Scala di Milano/Antonino Votto (2 CDs 5 56320 2)

La forza del destino (1954) – Tucker, Nicolai, Rossi-Lemeni/Coro e Orchestra del Teatro alla Scala di Milano/Tullio Serafin (3 CDs 5 56323 2)

Macbeth (live recording, Milan, 1952) – Mascherini, Tajo, Penno/Coro e Orchestra del Teatro alla Scala di Milano/Victor de Sabata (2 CDs 566447 2)

Rigoletto (1955) – Gobbi, Di Stefano, Zaccaria/Coro e Orchestra del Teatro alla Scala di Milano/Tullio Serafin (2 CDs 5 56327 2)

La traviata (live recording, Milan, 1955) – Di Stefano, Bastianini/Coro e Ochestra del Teatro alla Scala di Milano/Carlo Maria Giulini (2 CDs 5 66450 2)

La traviata (live recording, Lisbon, 1958) – Kraus, Sereni/Coro e Orquestra Sinfónica do Teatro Nacional de São Carlos, Lisbon/Franco Ghione (2 CDs 5 56330 2)

Il trovatore (1956) – Barbieri, Di Stefano, Zaccaria, Panerai/Coro e Orchestra del Teatro alla Scala di Milano/Herbert von Karajan (2 CDs 5 56333 2)

RECITALS

Maria Callas at La Scala
(Cherubini, Spontini, Bellini) (5 66457 2)

Lyric and Coloratura Arias
(Cilea, Giordano, Catalani, Boito, Rossini, Meyerbeer, Delibes, Verdi) (5 66458 2)

Mad Scenes
(Donizetti, Thomas, Bellini) (5 66459 2)

Verdi Arias, Vol. I
(*Macbeth, Nabucco, Ernani, Don Carlo*) (5 66460 2)

Verdi Arias, Vol. II
(*Otello, Aroldo, Don Carlo*) (5 66461 2)

Verdi Arias, Vol. III
(*I lombardi, Attila, Il corsaro, Il trovatore, I vespri siciliani, Un ballo in maschera, Aida*) (5 66462 2)

Puccini Arias
(*Manon Lescaut, Madama Butterfly, La bohème, Suor Angelica, Gianni Schicchi, Turandot*) (5 66463 2)

Rossini and Donizetti Arias (5 66464 2)

Mozart, Beethoven and Weber Arias (5 66465 2)

Callas à Paris, Vol. I
(Gluck, Berlioz, Bizet, Massenet, Gounod) (5 66467 2)

Callas à Paris, Vol. II
(Gluck, Bizet, Saint-Saëns, Gounod, Thomas, Massenet, Charpentier) (5 66467 2)

Maria Callas – The EMI Rarities
(Mozart, Verdi, Rossini, Bellini, Donizetti, Weber) (2 CDs 5 66468 2)

Maria Callas Live in Concert
(Puccini, Proch, Verdi, Donizetti, Delibes, Mozart, Meyerbeer, Charpentier, Rossini, Thomas, Wagner, Spontini, Bellini) (2CDs 5 72030 2)

Callas live in London 1958 & 1959
(Puccini, Rossini, Bellini, Boito, Verdi)(67912)

Callas Live in Paris 1958
(Bellini, Verdi, Rossini, Puccini) (67916)

Callas Live in Milan 9/27/5 and Athens 8/5/57
(Spontini, Bellini, Rossini, Thomas, Verdi, Wagner, Donizetti)

Maria Callas: In Rehearsal Dallas 1957
(67921-2)

Callas Live in Rome 2/18/52 and San Remo 12/27/54
(Verdi, Donizetti, Mozart, Meyerbeer, Charpentier, Rossini) (67922)

OTHER RECORDINGS

Callas La Divina
(Bellini, Gounod, Mozart, Puccini, Rossini, Saint-Saëns, Verdi)(54702)

Callas La Divina II
(Verdi, Bizet, Gluck, Charpentier , Thomas) (55016)

Callas La Divina III
(Delibes, Giordano, Leoncavallo, Massenet, Meyerbeer, Puccini, Rossini, Verdi)(55216-2)

Maria Callas At Julliard
(Mozart, Beethoven, Cherubini, Bellini, Rossini, Verdi, Massenet, Puccini)(65802)

Callas The Voice of the Century
(66628)

Italian Opera Duets – Callas, Di Stefano
(Verdi, Puccini, Bellini) (69543)

Maria Callas: Legend
(Bellini, Donizetti, Giordano, Puccini, Rossini, Saint-Saëns, Verdi)(57057)

The Very Best of Maria Callas
(Bizet, Puccini, Catalani, Saint-Saëns, Giordano, Mozart, Haydn, Verdi, (Cilea, Bellini, Charpentier, Ponchielli)(57230)

VIDEOS

Maria Callas – Life and Art (Documentary)
VHS 9 91151 2) (DVD 4 92248 9)

Maria Callas at Covent Garden (*Tosca*, Act II and arias from *Don Carlo* and *Carmen*) (VHS 4 91258 3)

Maria Callas – Débuts à Paris (Gala Concert 19 December 1958) (VHS 9 91258 3)

Maria Callas in Concert (Hamburg Concerts 1959 and 1962)
(VHS 4 91711 3) (DVD 4 92246 9)

$\mathcal{I}$ndex